Gimme Love . . .
Gimme Hope . . .
Gimme Shelter

The True Inspiration Behind the Movie
Gimme Shelter

by Kathy DiFiore

God Loves You!
K. DiFiore

Cover design by Mitchell Shea
Book design and production by Fedd Books, www.thefeddagency.com

Editing by Cara Highsmith,
www.highsmithcreativeservices.com
All photographs by Kathy DiFiore used by permission.

Translation:
Unless otherwise indicated, all scripture comes from the NIV translation.

Several Sources Shelters, Inc
PO Box 157
Ramsey, NJ 07446

Printed in the United States of America
First Printing, 2014
978-0-9894934-1-3
http://www.severalsourcesfd.org

DEDICATION

This book is dedicated to The Most Holy Trinity:

The Father who is the Creator of Life;
the Son, Jesus the Christ, who is Our Savior and Our Redeemer;
and, the Most Holy Spirit who is our Ever-Constant Companion if only we would ask it of Him—guiding us, and reminding us to:
"Ask and it shall be given to you; seek and you will find; knock and the door shall be opened for you."
—Matthew 7:7

This book is also dedicated to Our Lady of Guadalupe who appeared pregnant with the Child Jesus to Juan Diego in 1531.

Finally I share with you one of my favorite Bible Verses:

"Trust in the Lord with all your heart . . .
and He will make your paths straight."
(Proverbs 3: 5,6)

ARCHDIOCESE OF NEWARK
OFFICE OF CENSOR LIBRORUM
Rev. Msgr. Thomas Nydegger, Vicar General
171 Clifton Avenue
PO Box 9500
Newark, NJ 07104-0500

The publication described below has been examined:

Title of Book *Gimme Love...Gimme Hope...Gimme Shelter: The True Inspiration Behind the Movie* Gimme Shelter

Author Kathy DiFiore

Publisher Several Sources Shelters, Inc.

Address PO Box 157
Ramsey, NJ07446

Remarks no theological errors —

NIHIL OBSTAT Rev. Msgr. James M. Cafone

Date Sept 24, 2014

IMPRIMATUR +John J. Myers
+Most Rev. John J. Myers, D.D., J.C.D., Archbishop of Newark

Date 10/3/14

CONTENTS

Introduction

I never dreamed anyone would want to make a feature film about my life, but when the producers of *Gimme Shelter* offered, I knew God had a plan. God was working in my life, just as when I was honored by President Ronald Reagan at the White House and when I worked with Mother Theresa to change the laws in New Jersey to keep my home open to pregnant teens in need of shelter.

This book is not meant to be my memoir. Rather it is the backstory of what is portrayed in the film *Gimme Shelter* and what I think will be viewed by God as the most important moments of my life: helping young, abandoned, and confused mothers through their unplanned pregnancies.

Each chapter opens with a scene from the film *Gimme Shelter*, focusing on some words of wisdom Kathy shares with Apple. These are actual phrases I repeat constantly at Several Sources. They are messages I try to drive home with the girls.

My work started in my own home in 1981 when I invited that first pregnant teen to stay with me. My story is simple, yet complex. I, too, was abused and homeless once, and as I tried to pick myself up from the depths of my pain, sorrow, and loss of dignity, I found the only thing that seemed to help me was reciting over and over the Prayer of St. Francis of Assisi.

Prayer of St. Francis
Lord, make me an instrument of Your peace;
where there is hatred, let me sow love;
where there is injury, pardon;
where there is doubt, faith;
where there is despair, hope;
where there is darkness, light;
where there is sadness, joy.

O Divine Master, grant that I may not so much seek
to be consoled as to console;
to be understood as to understand;
to be loved as to love.
For it is in giving that we receive;
It is in pardoning that we are pardoned;
And it is in dying that we are born again to eternal life.
AMEN[1]

Whenever I would feel the despair return, I would go back to this prayer, and the Peace would slowly return to comfort me and bring me a life of renewed joy.

I began studying the life of St. Francis and learned that he built his life and his ministry around this passage in Matthew's Gospel:

> Then the King will say to those on his right, "Come, you who are blessed by my Father; take your inheritance, the kingdom prepared for you since the creation of the world. For I

1. http://www.catholic.org/prayers/prayer.php?p=134, last acces date 12/10/13

> was hungry and you gave me something to eat, I was thirsty and you gave me something to drink, I was a stranger and you invited me in, I needed clothes and you clothed me, I was sick and you looked after me, I was in prison and you came to visit me."
>
> —Matthew 25:34-36

I decided that since the Prayer of St. Francis helped me to heal, I also should follow his example by taking each and every part of this gospel message and making it a part of my life, so I made a checklist of three things to do.

My first step was bringing a very sick friend to live with me. She was suffering from Adult Acute Leukemia. As time passed, she slowly recovered and was able to move out on her own again.

I also began a small Prison Pen Pal Program for inmates at Rahway State Prison. That lasted three years, until the inmate who had helped me coordinate the inside pen pals was released. During this time, I was working on the third "To Do" list item, which was taking in a pregnant teenager. That was the joy-filled work my friends, family, and co-workers loved most. I had so much support pouring in for my efforts to assist frightened, abandoned, and often abused mothers and babies that I knew this was the right place to focus my energies.

That was in 1981. As the years have come and gone, thousands of women have passed through the Several Sources Shelters doors. Only God truly knows why a film was created about us. Throughout my thirty-plus years of serving pregnant women, I always chose to stay in the background, quietly serving these young mothers and their babies, but God now must have other plans.

Through a series of Divine coincidences and God's ability to "write straight with crooked lines," I met a young man named Ronald Krauss who would ultimately write, direct, and produce the film *Gimme Shelter*. My goal for this book is to explain the stories behind the story portrayed in the movie—the inspiration for what Kathy shares as she teaches the young mothers of the shelter and their family members. Some of what I cover here actually ended up "on the cutting room floor," as they say. Each chapter will open with an explanation of my philosophies and you will be introduced to one of the young mothers who currently lives, or has lived, at our shelters. You will see through these words how my inspiration, inter-woven with God's Holy Word, have helped these girls through their struggles. They are the words that have helped me through my own life. Throughout the chapters, as my life story unfolds, many of the young mothers share how they learn and deal with the responsibilities and blessings of motherhood. Our lives are entwined and I could not tell my story without including theirs as well.

"Dear Lord, as for myself, I ask nothing, except that You send me Your Most Holy Spirit so I may come to the knowledge of Your Holy and true will. Amen."

My prayer for you is that this book may help you too as you walk with Him every hour of the day. Always remember, He will if you but ask it of Him.

CHAPTER ONE

God Writes Straight with Crooked Lines

Every day our lives are filled with people and events that challenge us, bless us, and fill us with emotions. When counseling the mothers and the housemothers of our Several Sources Shelters, I will often say , "God writes straight with crooked lines."

This means we should seek God's Divine wisdom and guidance in every single thing He allows to happen to us. This helps to explain why 2,000 years ago when the apostles asked, "Lord, teach us to pray," Jesus responded with these words:

(Would you stop here and pray this most important prayer with me? The words are included for many reasons, but mainly because many of the young pregnant mothers who come to Several Sources Shelters for help do not know them.)

Our Father, Who art in heaven
Hallowed be Thy Name;
Thy kingdom come,
Thy will be done,
on earth as it is in heaven.
Give us this day our daily bread,
and forgive us our trespasses,
as we forgive those who trespass against us;
and lead us not into temptation,
but deliver us from evil. Amen.

—Matthew 6: 9-13[2]

Each of these lines is so very important that a separate book could be written about every line, but for now, let's focus on the words of Jesus the Christ which say, "Give us this day our daily bread."

Just yesterday I was on a conference call with five people to discuss a project they were working on. I asked if I could begin with a prayer. At first they seemed a bit reluctant, but one or two said, "Sure." As I prayed for the Holy Spirit to help us through the project, my heart was moved to mention a young, abused pregnant woman who was very desperately in need of a safe place to stay in Arizona. I simply could not get my mind off of Chastity and her most recent email to me explaining how all of the shelters in Arizona I had recommended to her were currently filled. And, so we all prayed.

After we closed the prayer, one of the participants mentioned that a young man named

2. http://justus.anglican.org/resources/bcp/1928/Family_Prayer.htm

Chris would be joining our call and that he lived in Phoenix and might be able to help. As I write these words, I am grateful to report that not only did Chris offer to help, but in a few short days this young woman will have a safe haven for her and her preborn[3] baby.

If I trace how many people and activities had to line up perfectly for Chastity to now have a home during her pregnancy and beyond, it simply would be more than I could explain.

The important thing here is to understand that God always sees the big picture. He knows our problems and when they will arise before we have a clue they are coming. So, when we put on and look through our "glasses of faith" we can clearly see His Divine hand guiding us every step of the way to a Holy Blessing. But we must recognize and give Him the credit or risk committing the original sin of pride. This is so very, very important. Always give God the credit for the good things that happen in your life. Even if, by some strange and almost impossible chance, God didn't send you the blessing, it doesn't hurt to give Him the credit and gratitude. Odds are really good there have been other times He has helped you when He didn't get the credit He so richly deserves. I like to think of this as giving God a reason to smile or to sing.

One day at our main shelter in Ramsey, New Jersey I was sitting at our dining room table working on a project. As I leaned over my work I

---

3. You will notice throughout the book that I use the term "preborn" instead of "unborn." I originally began using this term many years ago when I went to the "Cruise for Life" event hosted by the Greenwood Foundation. John Cardinal O'Connor asked the attendees to use "preborn." He thought the word would have a more positive impact on our society and culture versus "unborn," which does not sound as positive.

felt someone pass by me, moving toward the section of the shelter where the mothers and babies live. I remember hearing humming. There was no one there, but I sensed a presence and heard the humming. I know this might be a stretch, but at sixty-six years of age, with all I've seen, I don't think it's too much of a reach. I just knew in my heart that it was Our Dear Lord taking a moment in His unimaginably burdened day for what I like to call a "baby break." Amazing Grace, how sweet the sound!!!!!!!

Can you even imagine God humming? That's what He does when He experiences our love for Him and as He watches over us trying so hard to do His Divine will in these troubled and difficult days.

Pray for a few moments about how many times in your life when, in God's exact timing, problems were resolved. Think about the times you've encountered circumstances that were just so perfect that you were blessed to find a friend or the resources to achieve a goal that somehow healed your broken heart of a deep pain or suffering. And as you read these words, you may say, "Kathy, things like this just don't happen to me." Well then, I have a prayer for you to say from time to time:

Dear Lord,
Please take my eyes and replace them with
Your Divine eyes so I may see what You see.
Take my ears and remove them, so I can hear
with Your Divine ears and hear Your heart.
Take my heart and replace it with Your Most
Sacred Heart so I can feel what You feel.

Take my mind and replace it with Yours so I can think as You think and be inspired by Your Most Holy Spirit every hour of the day and live my life through the wisdom that You, Lord, alone can provide me.
AMEN.

Now, look back at even the most difficult of times when you thought, *Why ever did I have to meet this person? All he did was bring grief and suffering into my life.* When you think these thoughts, bring them to Jesus the Christ in the form of a meditation and sit in quiet to see if He inspires you with an answer. What did you learn from this negative experience? Was there a possible blessing that you have overlooked?

Can this crooked line—this mistake, this sorrow—through God's Divine grace and wisdom somehow become a blessing?

Darlisha

The first Several Sources Shelter mother I want you to know is Darlisha. She is not only featured in the *Gimme Shelter* film, but is a critical part of the real-life story as well.

Darlisha was eighteen years old when she found herself homeless and pregnant in freezing weather. She walked thirty-plus miles through the inner city streets of Newark, Irvington, and East Orange, New Jersey, and somehow found her way to our shelter in Ramsey.

Darlisha desperately needed a place to stay and we had one bed left, but we worked to find a solution. After an intake interview, the Housemother came to me and asked, "Should we accept her?"

These are the most difficult times to make the decision because once I say "yes" I lose the ability to shelter the next homeless, pregnant young mother. But I knew what I had to do. Then a thought came to me, *Why not let Ronald Krauss be the one to tell Darlisha "Yes, we have a bed!"?*

He was interviewing some of our Several Sources mothers for a possible documentary . . . And, the rest, as they say, "is history."

Ronald Krauss was coming to visit the shelter when he found Darlisha outside in the freezing January cold. He escorted her in, thinking she was a resident. She thought he was a member of our staff. Neither was correct. To my surprise, I found the two of them chatting when I arrived at the shelter.

Ronald explains, "When I told Darlisha she could stay, she tackled me and hugged me so hard, I thought I'd fall over." That was the night he got the vision for *Gimme Shelter*.

Darlisha is now twenty-two years old and has a beautiful son, Julian, who she has taught to call me "Grandma." When I asked her what she thought the phrase, "God writes straight with crooked lines," meant, she responded this way: "God has a purpose in your life, but not everything is going to be good or perfect. You're going to go through cracks, abuse, pain. Those are the crooked lines. But what's straight about God's writing is that there are lessons learned through the sufferings of those crooked lines.

"You learn how to help other people and learn how to cope with your life. You learn how everything is not going to be all glitter and gold. You learn these things by dealing with life issues—your past, your present and your future and being open about it and letting it go and releasing it and not letting it knock you down."

Darlisha stopped there as if wandering through the memories of her young life. I then asked her to give some advice to others who might read her words and she said, "If you pray and ask God for guidance and ask God to help you to forgive those who hurt you, and just listen for His guidance and allow Him to work in His ways in your life, then you will be able to have the crooked lines in your life be less."

I had to sit for a moment and absorb the comfort and the wisdom of her words. Once again, I heard the words, "Amazing Grace, how sweet the sound" in my heart. I wanted to continue our interview but was being inspired to share one of Jesus' miracles and so we took a little break. I read to her from Luke 8:43-48 about the woman who bled for twelve years and could not find anyone to heal her. Seeing Jesus in the road she found her way to him and touched the hem of his garment. She was healed immediately.

> And Jesus said, "Who touched Me?" When all denied it, Peter and those with him said, "Master, the multitudes throng and press You, and You say, 'Who touched Me?'" But Jesus said, "Somebody touched Me, for I

> perceived power going out from Me." Now when the woman saw that she was not hidden, she came trembling; and falling down before Him, she declared to Him in the presence of all the people the reason she had touched Him and how she was healed immediately. And He said to her, "Daughter, be of good cheer; your faith has made you well. Go in peace."
>
> —Luke 8:45-48

God was "writing straight with crooked lines" that day. Imagine the shock. She "snuck a miracle" from the Christ and with mercy and compassion, He sought her out to honor her and bless her with His comforting words, "Daughter, your faith has made you well; go in peace."

How many crooked lines did this woman have to travel to find Jesus in her life? How many doctors could not cure her? How many family members and neighbors simply gave up on her ever being healed? How many people in the crowd on that busy day did she have to navigate through before, she could but "touch the hem" of His garment? And what did these crooked lines of faith end up providing? A complete and immediate healing miracle!

She was bold and faith-filled enough to believe she could receive healing just by touching his robe. Her courage and faith was rewarded by Jesus Himself with a very public healing filled with a physical and a cultural blessing. The lessons to be learned from this miracle can touch all of our lives.

Simply put, we must have enough faith and courage to follow her brave example.

Likewise, Darlisha and all the young mothers of our Several Sources Shelters come with a tiny mustard seed of faith, or maybe no faith at all, seeking only the opportunity to give life to their innocent preborn children and become good mothers.

I am often asked, "What do you do for the mothers who come and live at Several Sources?" We have a full-time housemother at each shelter who is there to bond with the mothers, conduct nightly prayer, and provide for each individual mother's specific needs. All of our housemothers have support people they can turn to for help, guidance, and their own counseling if necessary. These include the Several Sources Manager of Maternal Child Care and a certified family counselor. Each of our mothers attends weekly counseling sessions to help them through individual and family problems.

We are there at the births of the babies to support and encourage the mothers. We provide birthing classes. Thanks to the generosity of one of our benefactors, we are able to provide for education beyond high school. We have a counselor who helps the mothers work to resolve family conflicts so they can be reunited with their loved ones. When their babies are sick, we act as their support system and as liaison with the clinic. The House Mother coordinates babysitting and provides childcare when the daycare is closed.

When a new mother brings her baby home, we give her the support she needs to heal and get acclimated to caring for her baby. The first six weeks are the most difficult. Beyond these basic services we strive to help our mothers make better choices as they achieve new goals and adopt new lifestyles as they learn about the Word of God and participate in Chasity workshops.

As I watch their love grow and see them mature into motherhood, I can only wonder what blessings God has in store for them through His divine mercy and compassion. I like to think we are acting as the hem of His garment, which they can touch and receive the miracle of His Love.

CHAPTER TWO

Stop Dancing with Your Demons

There is a scene in *Gimme Shelter* when a young woman named Apple is in Kathy's office worrying about her past problems. Kathy tries to help her realize that dwelling on these problems will not help her move in her future life as a young mother. In order to help Apple focus her energy on more positive thoughts, Kathy said to her these five words: "Stop Dancing with your demons." Do you remember the first time you ever danced with someone? What did the experience feel like? Was it fun? Romantic? Or was it awkward and embarrassing?

There is a saying, "If you can name it; you can tame it." That's part of what I try to do at our shelters with the young women who come to us. We ask them to be as honest as possible, and then, with lots of prayer asking for God's healing guidance, begin to move forward. We try to name whatever "demon" or negative energy is preventing them from peacefully walking with God. When these young women are able to identify that thing—whether it is past trauma, addiction, inability to forgive—and, then face it head on, they can learn to stop it from having power over them and their choices.

These mothers learn to ask God to walk with them and be a part of their lives as they face the temptations to get involved in destructive behaviors including drugs, lying, betraying a friend, cheating, or alcohol. Each girl will learn to ask God to walk with her as she makes choices that could destroy life.

I often give the book *This Present Darkness* by Frank Peretti to our young mothers and our housemothers to help bring to life the concept of how negative forces can truly change one's life. Peretti has a powerful way of introducing demons in his book. He gives each of the demons he introduces a specific name reflective of the negative quality the demon spreads to the people he is assigned to influence. For example Peretti uses the names, "Fear," "Harassment," and "Doubt." This concept has proven to be a helpful teaching tool with the mothers. Another book that helps explain the spiritual struggles we encounter is Joyce Meyer's *Battlefield of the Mind.* There are teen and kid versions as well. She shows us how to overcome the negative thoughts that interfere with the life God wants us to lead.

I think of when Jesus turned to Peter and said, "Get behind me, Satan! You are a stumbling block to me; you do not have in mind the concerns of God, but merely human concerns." (Matthew 16:23)

You see, Peter, in his humanity, tried to convince Jesus to defend himself and to take action that did not align with God's Divine plan. Peter did not understand Jesus' role as the Son of God and Our Divine Savior, and he ended up becoming a stumbling block to Jesus in what he was called to do. We face the same kinds of obstacles today. Satan and his evil spirits can influence others to take us off the path of the plans God has laid out for us. This is why we must pray every day, asking God to guide and protect us; to help us stay on His Path; to continuously walk with us, steering us through the challenges of our daily lives.

As I work with our young mothers and our housemothers, I speak about the power of prayer and remind them to ask for God's Holy Angels to surround them, their babies, and all of us at the Several Sources Shelters with their protection. I have noticed that people of all faiths are very open to the concept of Angels.

My friend Bill King, who helped me start the Several Sources Shelters, once had what he called a "meditation." In the meditation Bill was called by Jesus to come up to Heaven for a "visit." As Bill entered the heavenly room, he saw Jesus at something that looked like a large conference table. Around the table were angels and saints and in front of them on the table was what seemed like a set of architectural plans. Jesus looked up at Bill and welcomed him, but instead of asking Bill to join them at the table, Jesus instructed Bill to sit on a nearby couch. Jesus began a meeting about the current life of a particular man. As the meeting progressed, the various angels and saints discussed serious problems the man was experiencing in his life such as adultery and greed. One by one, the angels and the saints made suggestions on how to get the man's life back on the path to Heaven. God had put together this team with a mission and a critical purpose: where this man would ultimately spend eternity.

Now, the strange thing is that the mediation ended at that moment. Could it be that Jesus just wanted Bill to know how close He is to all of us, taking an interest in our plans and our goals, even when they are destructive and negative? Could it be that Our Lord wanted us to know that those are the moments when He assembles a team of Heavenly Hosts and Saints to help get us to refocus so we can get back on track?

When I share Bill's mediation with the Several Sources Shelter mothers, I discuss Heaven and Hell but the angels and the demons are what the mothers want to discuss the most.

Erika

Erika is seven months pregnant, thirty-four years old, and lives at our shelter. She has had a very difficult life filled with drug and alcohol abuse and with promiscuity. There is no need to detail her sufferings, but the sorrow of losing custody of her six-year-old son is something she must deal with every day of her life.

Erika explains:

I pretty much didn't have a childhood. My dad abandoned me when I was three years old and my mom was left alone to raise my brother and me. Mom was always working, so my brother basically looked after me. I admire my mother because she came to America from Portugal and is successful now. She did the best she could; but, instead of buying me things, I would rather she had spent time with me and been a more loving mom. Just a hug would have made me complete. I always felt like she favored my brother more and that made me feel like I wasn't good enough and that still follows me to this day. Why did she have to say, "Can't you be more like your brother?" That scares me and is what I hear when I hear the words "Stop dancing with your demons." My Demon is the demon of negativity. I think this is why I relive my childhood problems. I don't have my own identity because I keep asking myself if I can really be what she wanted me to be . . . . "more like my brother."

Then I got pregnant and I heard, "If you have this baby, you are going to be homeless." I can still hear those words to this day. How could I be homeless? I have a mom. I have a boyfriend that cares about me. So, it hit me just now, actually today, that I'm very fortunate to have—I don't know if I can call it my family—but people who are there for me. You know, that really care for you. So, this place has made me see and learn that. This is a game-changer, being here. It really is. It touched my heart to know that a total stranger is gonna love me and protect me and put a roof over my head and help me get an education. It's just things that my own family would never do for me and it really hurts.

I used to feel like I was "dancing with the demons" all the time. But now, I'm dedicated to school and learning and more focused and this has helped me to grow and be more independent and be more in control of myself and my life. My priorities have changed. I remember waking up and just wanting a drink. Now, I don't need that feeling of being in control of my life, that numbness. My faith is a lot stronger. Now I have a bond with God. I pray. It all happened when I decided to keep this baby. That was the day I left the clinic.

I was on the table and the nurse saw that I was upset. I remember she was wearing a cross and she said to me, "You don't have to do this." I turned and looked at the doctor. He stood there waiting and instead of giving me the needle to put me asleep, he said, "Make up your mind. I have a lot of women waiting out there." Then I looked in front of me and I saw at the end of the room a flood of white light and heard a voice that said, "Get out." I got up put on my clothes and left. That's when, in front of the building, I met a sidewalk counselor who brought me to the shelter and that day changed my life. It was like the old me just died and a new person was born. My relationship with my family is changing too. My mother is proud that I am studying and doing well in school. I thought this baby would cause drama and now my mother is thinking about moving back to New Jersey to be close to me and my daughter. So, keeping this baby has really changed my life and I have another chance to be a real family."

I tell the Several Sources mothers who are "dancing with their demons", to pray and ask God to help guide and strengthen them. This takes patience, forgiveness, humility, more prayer, and bible study.

In the Gospel of Mark (5:1-20), we are told about a demon-possessed man who lived in some tombs. No one could control him as he would "cry out and cut himself with stones." Was this man "dancing with his demons?" St. Mark continues to explain that when Jesus cast out the demon with the words, "Come out of this man, you impure spirit!," he asked the demon's name. The demon responded, "My name is Legion, for we are many." At the request of the demons, Jesus then gave them permission to go into a herd of pigs. "The herd, about two thousand in number, rushed down the steep bank into the lake and were drowned." When the healed man in his right mind wanted to follow Jesus, Jesus told him, "Go home to your own people and tell them how much the Lord has done for you, and how he has had mercy on you."

This is what we try to do at the Several Sources Shelters. We try to help our Dear Lord's healing process of the young mothers who come to us so that as they complete their pregnancies and begin to raise their babies into physically, mentally, and spiritually healthy children they will learn about how much God loved them while they were in their mothers' wombs, and how that love extends through every day of their lives. The progress can be slow; but, thanks be to God, we have the length of their pregnancies and beyond to work with them. While some of our mothers return home soon after their babies are born, most stay until they are able to live on their own and be independent. Even after they leave, if they need a helping hand, we tell them that they can always call because we are family and will be there to help them as long as possible.

Dancing with demons is not just a personal battle. Many times, the demons you come up against actually belong to some of the toxic people in your life. It could be a boyfriend or family member with an addiction or an abusive personality. It could be a person who simply can't be trusted. These people may be a key reason why a young mother will slip back into her prior lifestyle with all the problems of her past. We work hard to identify what negative influence friends and family members might have on mothers and equip them for resisting those pressures. This gives them room to become closer to God and His Holy Word. As their faith grows, the Holy Spirit inspires them and guides them to make healthy and holier life choices.

We also encourage each mother to understand what guardian angels are and how to identify them. We have an exercise that has become a tradition in our group meetings: I will ask the new members, "How many angels are present?" I'll ask the more senior mothers and the housemothers not to respond. The newer members of the group will count the people in the room and respond with that number. Once in a rare while a new mother will give the correct answer, but most of the time they miss the point I am making.

That is when a more senior mother, with a smile on her face, will raise her hand and count each pregnant woman twice—once for the mother and once for her preborn baby. Then it clicks and everyone nods their heads in agreement. Their eyes are open in wonder and awe at joining our new community of love, joy, and grace. At the Several Sources Shelters, we constantly remind our mothers that their their relationship with God is equally as important as having a healthy baby, for what would Heaven be like without having their sons or daughters with them too? We actually talk about the big parties we are going to have in Heaven where we expect everyone from Several Sources to be in attendance. On the walls will be photos of days gone by at the Several Sources Shelters and one of the highlights of the event will be a video of moments of our work and our activities that God thought were important and special to Him. You and your family are welcome to attend!!!

CHAPTER THREE

It's Okay. I Got You

Gimme Shelter portrays an unexpected visit from Apple's mother, June. As she leaves the shelter, she tries to take Apple with her. The scene is very intense. June slaps Apple so hard—it's hard to believe the girl could be still conscious. Kathy comes to Apple's defense and offers kind and comforting words as she helps her back into the safety of the shelter, "Its okay. I got you." These words stand for what we have become over these past thirty-three years—a safe haven from the cruel and unfair treatment our mothers have received simply because they wanted to have their babies.

Sadly, I can recall situation after situation over the years where pregnant girls ended up at my door because a disapproving parent threw them out of their home, or a boyfriend just couldn't cope with the responsibility and left her, or an abusive husband presented so much risk to her safety she feared for the life of her child.

One poor girl rang the bell on a rainy fall night, shivering from the cold, and simply said, "I'm pregnant and have nowhere to live. Will you help me?" All she had were the clothes on her back—no food, no money. A friend had heard about my home and dropped her off at my front door.

One pastor called with a parishioner's fifteen-year-old daughter who was told she could no longer live at home. We often get requests from churches, the police, and even hospitals with young women who need a place to live during their pregnancies and beyond. Numerous times we have been contacted by women who are sleeping in their cars and, as the cold winter months approach, they know their situation is endangering themselves and their preborn babies. There were middle-of-the-night calls to our hotline by a woman who was being pressured by her family to terminate her pregnancy. Thanks be to God we had more successes than failures in helping these poor girls.

The good news is that over the past three plus decades, we have experienced numerous times when a pregnant young woman who was cast aside by her family is reunited with them by the birth of the baby. In most cases, grandparents change their attitudes when their grandchild arrives. They want to see and embrace the addition to their family. They begin noting, "Oh he has Uncle Richard's ears," or "She has my mother's nose." And a family is restored in the love, mercy, and forgiveness of God's Holy and Divine plan. Happily, I can recall such a young mother not only coming to live at our shelter but eventually marrying her baby's father and they even had a second baby.

For every girl I am able to help, I am always haunted by the question: "Which girl do I turn away?" It keeps me up at night as I worry over this burden for women in need. This cross I have taken up is heavy as I am faced with the reality that I can't help everyone. I'm hopeful that as people read this book, they will feel led to open a shelter like ours. If so, they can go to www.severalsources.net to order a FREE How to Open a Shelter Kit.

When these women come to us, they are accompanied by another tiny soul—a brother or sister in Christ Jesus—who has yet to take their first breath of life. As the (Psalm 139: 13-14) states, "For Thou formed my inward parts: Thou didst weave me in my mother's womb. I will give thanks to Thee, for I am fearfully and wonderfully made."

Samantha

Samantha is one of those girls who weighed on my heart. She is one of those who was almost lost to us because of limited resources. She shares her story:

My mom moved to Tennessee with my brothers when I was sixteen. I just moved from friend to friend and worked odd jobs. I didn't get along much with her. We never really talked and were always arguing. Why? It's too complicated and not something I want to talk about. She had her reasons and so did I. It was just better we lived apart.

My friend found Several Sources Shelters on Google. I was eighteen and pregnant. I had no family or friends and I was trying to find other options. I was living in Florida and when the hotline counselor called all the shelters for pregnant women, she found out they were all filled. Then I got to meet a local Florida Several Sources volunteer. When they offered to fly me to New Jersey because they had an open bed, I wondered who these people were and what they were all about, but I decided to go and get a new start. I took a leap of faith getting on that plane. I was so scared. I didn't know who would be meeting me, but I felt like I had nothing to lose and everything had to be happening for a reason. When I got off the plane, not only was I in a new state, there was snow on the ground. I felt like I was on another planet. I was so scared. Soon after I moved in, my housemother came into my room and asked me to give everyone a try and she promised she would be there for me and my baby. She gave me a hug."

When I moved to Several Sources things really seemed strange—like everybody eating dinner together at the table. That was definitely weird. Why didn't you just get your food and go watch TV? When I first walked into the shelter, I saw the crosses and religious paintings everywhere. I thought, These people are REALLY Jesus people. *Now, I feel it is so good. I really like it. I even put a faith poster and a cross in my own room now.*

Before, when people said that they wanted to help me, I thought it was so strange. I remember my housemother would always come to my room and ask, "Are you okay? Do you want to talk? Do you need anything?"

I would hide everything, but now I know I can express myself and it makes me feel loved and happy. I now have someone who respects me and cares about me and my son and that is the best feeling in the world.

But, everything changed once I felt my baby kick me. It was then I knew I had a baby inside of me, something to live for besides me. I started coming out of my room and watching TV with the other mothers.

I was about four month pregnant. I was still scared and sometimes I would cry and then my baby would move. The doctor said, "You are stressing him out every time you cry." My son was trying to let me know he loved me. That's when I realized I needed to work harder to be happy and at peace for the both of us. Now, I feel it is so good that my son and I have all this help and care. I went from absolutely hating God and saying, "I talk to You and look what You do to me," to now praying to Him all the time.

Now I have somebody who is listening to me all the time—God. Every day. All the day long. When I'm sad or happy, he's with me every step of the way. He's like a full partner. You couldn't ask for any more than that. I'm so happy.

One of the requirements of the mothers of the Several Sources Shelters is participation in our weekly Bible Study. As with Samantha, each of our mothers grows in their faith during their stay with us. Jesus' parable of the mustard seed reflects this beautifully.

Jesus said, "What shall we say the kingdom of God is like, or what parable shall we use to describe it? It is like a mustard seed, which is the smallest of all seeds on earth. Yet when planted, it grows and becomes the largest of all garden plants, with such big branches that the birds can perch in its shade." (Mark 4:30-32). While a small parable, it truly captures the powerful spiritual growth of our young mothers in the critical virtue of faith.

Each girl faces their own challenges in relationships and adjusting to unexpected motherhood; but, some encounter other unforeseen obstacles, such as health problems in their child. Samantha explains the tests of faith she encountered:

When they told me that my son's kidneys were swollen and he might have Down Syndrome, I just looked at them. They wanted to do an amniocentesis and risk my son's life and said I might go into early labor.

I cried and I cried and got on my knees and I prayed so hard to God asking Him to help my son. Now he is fine. His kidneys were swollen, but now he is perfect.

They told me that my platelets were so low, like a fraction of where they were supposed to be. My platelets were completely normal the very next week. My doctors said to me, "Wow! how is that possible?" My platelets were at 35,000 and they should have been 200,000 and when I went back in one week they went to 190,000. The doctor said,

"It's a miracle. What are you doing?" I said, "Praying."

I went from having a hole in my heart and a stomach ulcer to being completely normal. My doctor said, "You are completely clear. This is the best thing I have seen in my life. Whatever you are eating, just keep eating it."

I knew it was just a change in direction that I had in my life. I went from nothing but complaining and thinking of my problems to praying because I had to. I went from doing things in my life just because I had too and being completely honest, I wanted to make things better for me and my baby. I hated everything and everyone. My health was down; my life was down. It's completely different now.

My mom and I have a better relationship. My mom apologized for all that she did to me. She came to visit me for four days after the baby was born. That was great. I cried for days when she left. Finally, I had my mom. She hugged me and explained everything to me. It hit my heart so deep. I just needed to hear so many things from her and they were said.

I always wanted to go to college. Now I have graduated and I can work with Autistic children and senior citizens. It is one step closer to where I want to be in my future for me and for my son. I'd say to the new moms: you are not alone. Friends come and go. You need to meet good people with no strings attached. Ask God to help you find people who say, "You help me, I help you!" You have to take a risk.

You are going to meet people who are going to show you a real family.

Samantha cried as she said, "I would tell a new mom that Several Sources is the best family you are ever going to have in your life." Samantha's tears and love for her son are simply as big a miracle as the physical healings they both experienced during her time at the Several Sources Shelters. No one, including her doctors, could explain how diagnosis after diagnosis was followed by healing for both of them. I often say there are no atheists in Labor and Delivery rooms. And that's where a mother's faith grows in God—as she holds her baby for the very first time. Their maternal love is a miracle I get to watch and participate in on a daily basis. Motherly love is the cornerstone and the hope for the future of our culture. Together with the help and guidance of God's Most Holy Spirit, we must continue to do all things possible to secure a positive foundation for young women and their babies.

Just when I think I'm finished with a chapter, something develops that I have to share! I recently received an email from Samantha so beautiful that I know needs to be included in this book.

> Hello to all.
> I'm writing this to inform you all that me and Noah will be leaving Several Sources in the first two weeks of December. I want to thank each one of you for all that you have done for me. But more importantly what you

have done for my son. I remember coming here February 5th so scared and lost. Trying to have faith but not really knowing what that meant. Thinking that I was a strong woman, because I never broke down. But now looking back, I honestly had no idea. Moving to Several Sources was the best thing that I could have ever done with my life. It's taught me what a strong woman really is—to take on the world with no fears. It taught me that God is great and no matter how rough my days get he's always by my side. Being here has taught me how to be a mother and what love is. What the true meaning of love is and all it stands for. I came here broke down, physically, mentally, and emotionally. And now I'm leaving stronger than I've ever been and happier than I ever thought was possible. I can't thank you all enough for saving me and my baby. With my CNA and my head screwed on straight I'm completely ready to leave back home to Florida, to show my family that I am somebody and I made it. I plan to keep in touch and remain a part of the Several Sources family. No matter how far I am.

God bless you!
Samantha[4]

4. Samantha learned on December 7th that she passed her CNA (Certified Nursing Assistant) exam and now has her license, which is transferable to the state of Florida.

Samantha will always be a part of our Several Sources Family.

CHAPTER FOUR

Don't Cast Your Immaturity on Me

In *Gimme Shelter*, Kathy meets with Apple to go over the rules of the shelter. They discuss her family, her status as a minor, and what that means for staying at the shelter. Kathy explains that she must have the consent of a parent for her to remain at the shelter because Apple is a minor. Apple becomes angry, calling Kathy a "liar." Rather than allowing the situation to devolve, Kathy simply states, "Don't cast your immaturity on me."

With my undergraduate degree in psychology and my thirty-plus years of living and working with our Several Sources mothers, I have come to understand that many times our young mothers who are often emotionally and/or physically abused simply lash out at us because they have learned such behaviors from others. They project their negative feelings on us, not even understanding that they are doing so. Over time and through God's healing graces, our mothers learn how to process and heal past wrongs as they learn to forgive and

grow into the mothers God intends for them to become.
St. Paul explains spiritual growth in 1 Corinthians 13: 11-13.

> When I was a child, I spoke as a child, I understood as a child, I thought as a child; but when I became a man, I put away childish things. For now we see in a mirror, dimly, but then face to face. Now I know in part, but then I shall know just as I also am known. And now abide faith, hope, love, these three; but the greatest of these is love.

Thalia

But what happens to a young mother who doesn't really experience love in her childhood? How can this wounded little dove come to know, love, and serve God and her child? This is a major part of our Several Sources mission. Together with the help of God's Most Holy Spirit, we travel a modern day road to Emmaus. Permit me to explain this biblical comparison in more detail after I share with you Thalia's story.

Thalia was born in New Jersey and grew up in Middletown, New York. Her parents divorced when she was a small child and she had a younger brother. She explains,

The hardest part of growing up was not having a father around much. Then I was in and out of one foster family's home for about three years. Finally, I moved for a year into a condo with my dad and his

family. Somehow Social Services was involved. I don't remember it all. I was a kid. But, then my dad lost custody to my mother who also lived in New York State.

I don't know why, but my mom and I did not really talk much. I only remember in my whole childhood us having one Christmas tree. No presents, not even on our birthdays. Wait, I remember having a birthday cake once when I was ten years old. Actually, now that I think of it, we never even had a turkey on Thanksgiving. She said it was against her faith. . . . Wow, I'm just realizing this for the first time now.

I think my mom had mental problems. She had two personalities. She had her good side and her bad side. I remember a time things got pretty bad. A police officer came to our house and they almost took me away from my mom. She came from the mental hospital to our house. The police came and said, "Would you like your mom to come back home?" We said yes because my brother and I had no other choice.

My brother left home earlier than me. I left at eighteen years when I had an opportunity to share an apartment with a friend.

My mom worked as a Home Health Aid for elderly people on and off, with welfare and food stamps. I worked at two jobs from sixteen until I got pregnant with Jonathan who was born Jan. 31, 2004. Jonathan's father walked away as soon as he found out I was pregnant. He didn't want anything to do with the baby.

I was living with my aunt at the time and she kicked me out because I was pregnant. Because I was working two jobs, I could afford to live at a motel for two weeks. I found Several Sources through Social Services and I moved in the very next day. I felt safe and comfortable while I continued to work and go to technical school. The strangest thing about coming to the shelter was that I thought it would be a bunch of cots or beds in a big room, and instead it was like a normal house and it was safe. I worked and went to school just about up until I gave birth. The toughest part of being a mom was when he was a baby and he had some problems walking; but, after some physical therapy, he was perfectly fine. Now he loves sports and plays soccer and floor hockey.

My childhood makes me feel a little sad because sometimes I don't even know how to pass this along to my own children how to celebrate. I have that by being here. The housemothers taught me and even came with me to go to a soccer game with us or go to the Pre-K graduation or a Halloween Party. My mother gave me one birthday cake when I was ten and that was it. There was no love in it because she would complain about my friends all the time. I can't figure out why. Basically, she said it was her faith that told her not to celebrate anything but the birth of Jesus Christ. But every year at Several Sources has been a big help for me since the boys were born because they have taught me how to celebrate and enjoy many other things.

I learned how to celebrate special days with Kathy and my housemothers. They would come with me to Jonathan's school and sports events. We would always be celebrating a baby's birth or the 4th of July or something special. This taught me how to celebrate now in my own family.

That was just the beginning of my family life, because I met my future husband shortly after Jonathan was born and the next thing you know, I was married with two boys! Now I work for Several Sources as Kathy's assistant and both my sons—Jonathan (age 10) and Brandon (age 7)—and my husband (Jose) are all proud members of the Several Sources Family. My dad has even become a part of our family. Four years ago he stopped by and since then he's been interested in the boys and what's happening to us all. What was a broken family is now fixed.

My relationship to God has changed because of my life at Several Sources. We go to church together. Every night before they go to bed we pray together and every day when we sit down to eat, we pray. Last year Jonathan completely surprised me when he wrote this Christmas note:

Dear God,

Thank you for my life. You made my life awesome. You are awesome. I wish I can see you but I cannot. I learn about you in church. Thank you for my mom. If she was not here, I would not be here. I will try better at school. If you see this, please write back.

Luv,
Jonathan

Many of our young mothers seem to have one thing in common: fathers who were missing during their childhoods. The question is: can we, by introducing Our Dear Lord in the Most Holy Trinity to whom this book is devoted, somehow serve Him in healing the wounds of a missing earthly father?

Can a fatherless child who is now a young woman and a mother pray to have the hole in her fatherless heart filled by God's Holy Graces? Again and again we must, like the two apostles on the road to Emmaus, help these young mothers to realize that they are not alone.

Our Lord and Savior is with them every single step of their life's journey. We must help them through our prayers and our example of faith and love to feel the inspirational message that the disciples experienced as they walked with Jesus.

In Luke 24:25-26, we learn of two disciples who were traveling to Emmaus after Jesus' crucifixion. A stranger joined them on the road and talked with them as they walked. They told him about their loss and who Jesus was. They explained how His body had been removed from the tomb, adding to their grief. At this point, the stranger says to them, "O foolish ones, and slow of heart to believe in all that the prophets have spoken! Ought not the Christ to have suffered these things and to enter into His glory?"

Once they reached the village, they begged Him to stay the evening with them. While they were having a meal together, they saw who this stranger was. It was their Lord. They returned to Jerusalem the next day to spread the word that Jesus had, indeed, risen. They explained how he had walked with them all along the journey and how their eyes were opened when they sat together to break bread.

Do you think the young mothers like Thlalia, Darlisha, Samantha, and Erika who have the courage to have their babies are also worthy of having Jesus walk with them throughout every hour of their days as His daughters?

He walked with the Apostles 2,000 years ago, and after His death on the cross and resurrection from the dead, He returned not only to His apostles but these two disciples on the road from Emmaus, maybe simply to inspire us to trust Him to walk with us every hour of our day and to let us know we are not alone in any single minute of our lives. He is as near as our heartbeat . . . if only we ask it of Him.

Read and read again the words of Luke's Gospel for the Emmaus message. What does this passage mean to you personally? Think of how God's Most Holy Spirit touches your very soul when you read Luke's words; "In addition, some of our women amazed us. They went to the tomb early this morning but didn't find his body. They came and told us that they had seen a vision of angels, who said he was alive."

I have seen so many miracles happen in the lives of these girls that seem impossible—the voice that spoke to Erika encouraging her to get up and leave, Thalia's change of heart, or Samantha 's healing. Yet, Jesus Himself said, "With man this is impossible, but with God all things are possible." (Matthew 19:26). Thus we can have so much hope in our daily walks with Him. Together let us pray,

As you walk with God today, pray every step of the way. Become the prayer and watch your life change for the better. As together we ask for, *All His Holy Angels and Saints and the Blessed Virgin Mary to join us in our, AMEN.*

CHAPTER FIVE

Learn to Cooperate

There is a moment in *Gimme Shelter* when Apple is in Kathy's office that demonstrates how both of them clearly live in different worlds. Kathy is the founder and director of a unique shelter for pregnant teens while Apple is a runaway with no real future and a baby due in a few short months. Kathy's responsibility is to equip each of the residents as they come into a very difficult world and community. As *Gimme Shelter* unfolds, the audience learns with Kathy that "cooperation" is difficult to come by in today's dark and often dangerous world of teen pregnancy.

How does one learn to work with others when all they've known is conflict? How can they believe there is help out there when they have had no one to turn to in these most fearful and complicated of circumstances? What does one do when they have been robbed of their childhood by parents' drug addiction, violence, and abuse?

When our shelters first opened in the early eighties, I took in so many mothers who were broken and abused, confused and downhearted, I was inspired with this beautiful meditation to share with the young women:

My Salvaged Soul

Even as the poor walk slowly through the refuse dumps, bent over, looking for a bit of something of value, so also does Christ Jesus in Spirit walk slowly through the spiritual wreckage of our lives. From time to time, He kneels and sifts through the sinful, tortured souls and broken promises to Him and Christ picks up a lonely, wounded, little soul—a broken gift from God, a treasure among the trash, a soul, long lost to the child of God who first received it at the moment of conception, a soul neglected and abandoned by all, save God.

I had thought my sins so great as to bar my soul at Heaven's gate. I hid my soul where none could see, among those hopeless, lost, like me. For I had thought my soul to be too sinful, torn, and tattered—beyond redemption.

But Christ Jesus has a plan. Kneeling, He lifts my worthless soul in His nail-pierced hands. The Blood of the Lamb washes the sin from my soul. Christ cups my soul into His hands and gently brings it to His Sacred lips. He breathes His Holy Spirit into my soul.

> Christ holds my soul up high above the Crown of Thorns that pierces and bloodies my Savior's brow. As one would release a dove to flight, Christ frees my soul, "Fly little soul, fly far and high. Let the love I place within your heart and faith that I place within your soul draw other souls to Me. For I have abandoned none who sin. I wait patiently among the lost souls to help, to heal, and to save all. I am here among you, my children, yea, even unto the end of time. Amen.

So many of our Several Sources mothers feel these words are a blueprint of their young lives. Perhaps you may as well. And, for some of my mothers, such as Lana, their innocence is taken from them. She never wanted her mother and father to become drug addicts. She was nine years old when she and her brother and sister were sleeping in cars, abandoned houses, or garages and taking care of themselves. Her grandmother decided the only way to break Lana's mother's drug addiction was to send her to Mexico without documentation. Thankfully, Lana's mother is now drug-free and married with a two-month-old boy named Jose. But, Lana and her siblings suffered throughout their childhood.

Lana describes how the three children moved in with their aunt when Lana was twelve.

Living there was difficult because all she wanted was the money. We never had new clothes. She didn't care. She didn't love us or give us the most basic things. All she wanted was the money for herself.

She would throw things at my face and yell, "You're just going to be like your mother and father. I'm smarted than you."

At the beginning, my family was going to church. That was before my dad was using drugs. When he stopped going to church, he started drugs again. So God was out of my life.

My dad took me from my aunt's house when I was thirteen years old. My dad began to rape me from when I was fourteen. It was a continuous thing for a year. Everywhere he went, I had to go. He had me on lockdown. I couldn't leave the house. I remember when he was doing that to me that he was on drugs. He said that I was "helping him." I still don't know what that means.

That's when I saw a black shadow, very dark and very scary. It looked human but very evil. I was very surprised to see it. I didn't want to tell my father anything. I thought it was the devil. But I told my father and he said, "He's not here for you. He's here for me."

When I was fifteen years old, I ran. We were in the car in Pomona, CA. I had enough of everything he had done to me. I jumped out of the car while it was moving. I ran as far as possible. I called this lady that was my father's friend. They did drugs together. She was always nice to me.

I cried and she hugged me and told me, "This is never going to happen to you again. I'm not going to force you to do anything you don't want to do. But do what you think is right." I was only fifteen years old. I was tired of it all. I knew my father was looking for me. I was scared that he would find me and do something to me.

I was scared to get beat up again. You have to stand up for yourself and be strong. I called the police and told them what my father was doing to me. They put him in custody and then jail for about three years because he confessed. My aunt heard what happened, but when I got back home, she didn't do anything different.

She said, "I told you he was bad. You should never have moved in with him." She knew he was hitting me. I didn't tell anyone because he was always with me, checking my computer and my cell phone.

Instead of dealing with me, my aunt sent me to my mother in Mexico for six months. I didn't want anything to do with school. I just wanted to be on drugs myself. But Mexico just helped me realize California had much more to offer; so, I came back to California and started to go to school and get better grades, and little by little things began to change.

I see being raped was the biggest thing that ever happened to me. I just had to think about how I was still alive, because there are many girls that aren't just raped; they are murdered, too. But then I got raped again when I was eighteen. I didn't even know it happened. I was at a party and six weeks later I was in the hospital and the doctor was telling me that I was pregnant.

All my family told me they would not support me having this baby because I wasn't ready. I was eighteen. They said that they wouldn't let me back into the house until I was no longer pregnant and that they were not going to help me if I was going to have this child. They said, "There will be no place to stay, no money for you or this child." That was all I heard over and over again.

My best friend went with me into the clinic. We both agreed that this was the thing to do. But then when I was inside I just pictured this little baby running around calling me and laughing. I couldn't see myself staying at the clinic any longer so I left. I dropped all the papers and got out of there as fast as I could.

I thought, Maybe it's time for me to change the cycle and be a good mother? *Then my girlfriend went on the Internet and found Several Sources Shelters in New Jersey. I kept saying, "How are these people going to help me? There is no possible way that people in New Jersey are going to help me in California. I just can't believe this. The whole thing is CRAZY."*

My Several Sources counselor's name was Jasmine. First, she tried finding shelters out in California. The only ones that had openings were ones that would only let you stay for thirty days and I was already jumping from house to house. So, one day she asked me if I would like to come to New Jersey. Some benefactor said he would fly me out there and I would live with total strangers, free food, free housing. I thought, These people are insane.

Jasmine said, "Why don't you come stay with us for a week and check it out. Trust me." I don't know why, but I decided to trust her. It took me awhile. She called me about five times. I avoided her phone calls, but my friend thought I should try it. So, I did.

When I met Virginia and Nancy at the airport in New Jersey, they seemed nice. I really thought maybe they only wanted my baby. I had to see all the other girls with their babies. Watching the moms with their kids for about a month helped me to understand and believe that this place is for real.

The toughest part was leaving my brother and sister behind. I miss them. But the best part is getting away from so much negativity in California. I now feel brightness and the light inside of me. My good friend lives in Pennsylvania. She was the one who found this place on the Internet for me. She comes and visits me and even was there when I gave birth to my baby.

My precious Liliana was born on Oct, 22, 2013. My daughter means the world to me. I can look at her and smile, and most of the time I want to cry, not tears of sadness, but tears of joy. I feel that she is the best thing that has happened to me in my life. When I first saw her, I thought it was crazy. This baby came out of my stomach. I just couldn't believe; I just kept repeating, "That's my baby." I know she loves me so much. I love her so much, because she's the best thing that ever happened to me. I thanked God so much and promised Him that

I'm going to be the best mom ever to her. The biggest challenge ahead for me will be to let go when she grows up. She will eventually have to be by herself and I'm scared for her to be alone.

Her father is not part of this because he told me not to have this baby and he didn't want anything to do with it. He took advantage of me—I didn't even know I had sex until six weeks later when I found out I was pregnant. My friends thought I was okay. They had seen me with him talking as friends. That's all I remember. They didn't realize I was out of it. They thought I was a willing participant. I decided not to go to the police. The guy had a wife and a child AND a kid with another woman. I didn't want to ruin their family.

I had my first panic attack when I was eighteen. I was told by mistake that my father was out of jail. I just was so scared. I had my second panic attack when I found out I was pregnant. I was in shock. Then again when I got to New Jersey. All the moms, babies, and housemothers were at this diner and I had another panic attack. I ran outside and Kathy came looking for me. I remember her taking off her coat and wrapping it around me in the parking lot. I honestly don't know how she found me. She was gently just holding me and rocking me until I stopped shivering. She somehow found a way to calm me.

I remember going to church with my best friend when I went to go visit her. I was eight months pregnant and I was sitting there and the pastor was talking about God saying, "You're not alone. You are here. He has a future for you. Forget your past and He has you here now for a reason. I felt that touch me in a way, because I was stuck in my past. When I came to the shelter I was miserable. I wanted my family and I didn't know this child. When I went to that church, the pastor was talking about forgetting your past. "You have a future now today and I want to tell you I love you." I thought that this is crazy, because I personally felt like God was talking to me through the pastor.

We have Bible study here and that is a good thing. It gets us to know more about God and what He does for us. The stories in the bible help us to know more about how He works. I pray every day. I talk to him all the time—in the shower, when I'm doing dishes. My relationship got stronger when I moved here. I believe He listens to me. He shows me His ways in the love and care from people around me here at Several Sources—so He is giving me that love and the care that I ask for.

My biggest concern is what am I going to teach my daughter about men? It is going to be difficult for me to even let her talk to men. I really wanted to have a boy. But, I'll be asking God what to say and I'm sure He will help me.

This place is very different—like having a family that cares for you and loves you and doesn't judge you. They are just like a true family that you see on TV and you don't actually think that kind of family really exists.

This baby means the world to me and, if this shelter had not been here, she would have never been here, because I wouldn't have been able to give her a home and I thank everybody here. I couldn't have done it without anybody and the help that I get here. These shelters need to stay open to help the many other women who really want to keep their babies. And those that think they don't but they actually do. The reason most girls want to come to a shelter is because they feel they don't have family to support them. These shelters give support, care, and love, and they show you that you're not alone. And that's what many girls need out there in their life.

I would say to a girl who needs a place to come, if you get invited here, come because God is opening up a place for you and this is it.

While my interview with Lana took only ninety minutes, her words and her life story will stay with me for all eternity. She had been violated not once, but twice, yet she found enough compassion to let her pain and suffering go as she moved on with her life.

Lana's story reminds me of when Jesus said, "Whoever causes one of these little ones who believe in me to sin, it would be better for him if a millstone were hung around his neck, and he were drowned in the depth of the sea." (Matthew 18:6)

Lana showed a level of mercy and forgiveness while so very young that many of us never understand. She is growing into the role of a loving young mother—one any daughter would be proud to call her own. Lana had such few positive role models in her childhood. The support of our housemothers and staff has helped her with the guidance and nurturing she needs. She found a shelter that met her immediate need, but she also receives a heartwarming family and a dependable support system, which will help shape her future.

Lana commented, "I believe that more shelters should be out there everywhere—New Jersey, California, Mexico—anywhere it's possible, because there are so many girls out there going through so many evil things. They don't know what to do when they end up pregnant. That baby could've come from a guy they never even knew, and it's hard for them already going through something alone."

Lana takes to heart the words, "Forgive them their trespasses" and it is her forgiving nature that will free her from her past.

In January 1991, Mother Teresa wrote me a lovely letter. Part of her words relate to Lana's pureness of heart,

> "Let your humility continue to radiate the greatness of God. How wonderful are His Ways! He uses humility, poverty, smallness, and helplessness to prove to the world, that He loves the world – that He loves you and me today. So let us not be afraid to be small, humble and helpless to prove our love for God." [5]

What an amazing insight into this young woman's very soul. Mother Teresa wrote these words over twenty years ago—healing words that have helped guide Lana and all of us today. What a gift!

---

5. Images of all letters from Mother Teresa are included in the photo insert.

I am honored to say I know Lana, and through God's mercy, grace, and divine compassion, all of us at the Several Sources Shelters try to be a source of His strength, His peace, and His joy as she continues to grow as a loving and caring mother.

When Our Dear Savior hung on the cross He looked to his disciple John and then said to His mother, Mary, "Woman, here is your son." (John 19:26) Jesus created a bond between His own mother and all of us, His followers, to this very day.

One of my favorite visions of Our Blessed Mother, Mary, is Our Lady of Guadalupe (1531) where she appears to Juan Diego comforting him by enfolding him in her mantle and saying, "Hear and let it penetrate into your heart, my dear little son: let nothing discourage you, nothing depress you. . . . Am I not here who am your mother? Are you not under my shadow and protection? Am I not the source of your fountain of life? Are you not in the folds of my mantle, in the crossing of my arms? Is there anything else that you need?"[6] What could be a more tender moment for a child looking for his or her Mother's nurturing support?

For me, the most interesting aspect of this apparition is that Mary appeared dressed with a brown sash which was the sign in the village of Guadalupe at that time that she was pregnant with the Baby Jesus!!! She is also the Patron Saint of the Americas. What a fitting icon for Lana and all pregnant women and their little ones in need of our support!

---

6. http://catholiceducation.org/articles/stories_of_faith_and_character/cs0092.html

Join me in the meditation honoring Jesus the Christ, who is available to us every hour of the day:

Think not that you exist on earth alone.
Think not that you leave the earth alone.
For this is not the truth.
For He that created all men will walk beside you if you but ask it of Him.
For He that is the Father of all mankind shall spend each hour of the day with you, if you ask it of Him.
For He that is the Giver of Life to all men, for He that is the Hope and the strength of all mankind for He that so loved mankind as to give the life and blood of His only Son, so as mankind shall find everlasting life in His Kingdom when he passes from this earth, the Lord God of Heaven shall not leave you, if you but ask it of Him.
Amen.

CHAPTER SIX

I'm Sorry. I Made a Mistake.

In the film Kathy runs into a serious problem. Apple is a minor and neither parent has given permission for her to live at the Several Sources Shelters. Kathy explains to Apple that she could be face prosecution for kidnapping Apple and risk losing the shelter if they can't get one of her parents to approve. Apple feels betrayed when her mother and father come to the shelter to meet with Kathy. Kathy hoped to resolve the problem with a face-to-face meeting, but chaos unfolds and she realizes it was a bad idea trying to meet with Apple's parents together. She says, "I'm sorry. I made a mistake," and shuts down the conference.

Families are complex and when an unmarried daughter of any age comes home pregnant, even the best of families can find themselves at odds with society, with other family members, and their faith.

The Bible recognizes the complicated relationships we can have with our families. In Mark 3:23-25 Jesus tells us: "How can Satan drive out Satan? If a kingdom is divided against itself, that kingdom cannot stand. If a house is divided against itself, that house cannot stand."

Disagreement over how to handle an unplanned pregnancy is destructive to families when mothers are forced to choose between their loved ones and the leading of the Holy Spirit.

If you are reading this book you may know or have known a pregnant teen or an unwed mother. In my thirty-plus years of experience helping pregnant teens and other pregnant women, I have learned that unplanned pregnancies most definitely can divide families. The ongoing need expressed through our hotline, our websites, and our shelters is evidence that this conflict still dominates our society. Our hope is to bring resolution to the issues that keep families in turmoil over the choice of life for preborn babies.

There are varying statistics on teen pregnancy, births, and the termination of pregnancies. All reporting is voluntary and, therefore, subject to interpretation. However, we do know that hundreds of thousands of girls are getting pregnant each year and a staggering number of them terminate their pregnancies—in most cases because they believe they have no hope and no options. This is why we exist and why we are constantly seeking support for the work we do. An unplanned pregnancy does not have to mean the voluntary loss an innocent baby or the end of the world for their mother. For anyone who finds themselves in this situation, please look for resources like Several Sources Shelters to help you give life to your precious child.

Over the years we have seen mothers as young as eleven years old and as old as forty! No matter the age, these women need support and a place to stay to help them complete their pregnancies. I have noticed two dramatically different responses to unplanned pregnancy—while many more families are accepting their daughters' pregnancies and allowing them to remain at home, the extreme opposite is also true. Too many young women are battered, abused, humiliated, harassed, and lied to by the people around them.

We have counseled too many young pregnant women who have been "forced" to make choices about the future of their babies simply because the fathers or their families did not want the baby to be a part of their lives—such a tragedy when so many families are waiting desperately for a child to adopt.

As I write this book, I have a seventeen-year-old I am trying to help whose mother had locked her in her bedroom and had her younger sister guard her until she agreed to go to the clinic. We had only text messaging to work with since the mother had taken away her computer and email; but, day-by-day, this young teen held her ground and absolutely refused. Eventually, the angry mother stopped trying to force her into this decision. Her screaming and harassment continued for days, but eventually stopped. Her baby boy (Brian) is due to be born in a month and all is good. She has found peace in their family. Thanks be to God!!!

I remember sitting in the Several Sources living room last summer and looking at the black and blue marks on the shoulder and arm of one of our mothers. I asked, “How did that happen?” The young woman responded, “Remember, I told you my mother pushed me down the steps hoping I would lose the baby?” I was shocked.

Unfortunately, we are not always able to rescue girls or help reconcile them with their families. I counseled a young woman who lived near Philadelphia, PA. She was so afraid of her father and his temper that no matter what I said or what her baby’s father or his parents said, there was nothing we could do to help her resolve the family conflict. She decided not to continue her pregnancy and all we could do was offer her information about follow-up counseling (which you will find in our resource list in the back of this book).

Monet

I’d like to share with you Monet’s Story. She was sixteen and pregnant.

I asked my basketball coach to go with me to get the pregnancy test and then help me tell my mother. I knew her since I was in fourth grade. When my coach and I showed up, my mother guessed that I was pregnant and said, “Okay, we’re going to take care of it.” She asked me why didn’t I tell her and I said I thought she was going to yell at me.

Then my coach left and my mother called the clinic to make the appointment. My mother called my boyfriend’s mother and told her. She said that she would go to the clinic and that my boyfriend would go to the clinic too. My mother kept asking me why didn’t I tell her and I just didn’t answer her.

A couple of days later we were all at the clinic and they told me everything that they were going to do to me because I was already five months. For example, they told me they were going to put something in my cervix and I would have to come back the next day for the procedure. I asked what was it that they were putting in me and they showed it to me on the computer. It was this little silver thing. The doctor explained what she was going to do.

I'm so glad I didn't do it. I don't really know how I feel about it. They tried to convince me and they kept trying to convince me but I said no! I sneaked a quick look at the sonogram picture and my own feelings were that the baby is big. That made me want to keep my baby. I asked the doctor, "Can I see the sonogram picture?" She said, "No, I'm already done." But, since I peeked already, I just knew what I had to do.

I know I was so strong because God gave the strength to say no to my mom and be strong for my baby. I was sad that I was going to let my mother down, but somehow God just gave me the strength to.

I would say to any girl, "Don't let anyone pressure you into doing it, because God is on your side and He will help you through any struggle you may have. It is your decision.[7]

My mother surprised me and found Several Sources by speaking to a crisis pregnancy center. She was mad and said to me that I was making a

---

7. Go to the back of this book for instructions on how to continue your pregnancy with proper support, whether you are a minor or not. Now here are the exact links: http://www.lifecall.org/stop-your-abortion.html

stupid decision. She's not mad any more. She's very happy I decided to keep him.

The next day after I left the clinic, my mother dropped me off at Several Sources Shelter. I came with my bags. She said she would keep in touch and drove off. The first person I meet was my housemother.

When I first moved in I liked it. It was like a regular home and other mothers were cool and nice. I went to 10th grade. I didn't like it. They would stare at me because I was the only black person there and the only pregnant person there. But, I did well in my grades at the end of the year. It was a good experience and it taught me how to be a mother. They taught me about chastity. The bible studies were good and the bible-based videos were my favorites.

The most difficult part of my pregnancy was telling my mother because every time we saw a pregnant girl she would tell me to wait until I was married before I had sex. I would say tell your mother. Maybe she will be disappointed in you, but don't be afraid because the baby comes first. If you are thinking of not having your baby and going instead to a clinic, please stop and think, because there are other things you can do like you can place the baby for adoption or do an open adoption where the mother gets to see her baby once in a while and write and send photos back and forth to the adoptive mom and dad, so they can still be a part of their child's life.

Right now I do miss some things like going out with my friends, but I don't care, because my son comes first. When I look at him I'm so glad I left that clinic. I always knew I didn't want to do it, but I was afraid that maybe my mom was going to make me. But God definitely gave me the strength. I just asked God to keep him healthy and safe. God has answered all my prayers.

Gregory Sr. loves his son. He and his mother take care of him when I'm at school. He is with his father and his father's mother Monday thru Saturday and his father even changes his diapers. He actually sensed I was pregnant before I knew it. My boyfriend always wanted me to have the baby. When I was living at Several Sources Shelters, I used to ask my mother, "Please let me come home." She saw a big change in me, but what really changed her mind was when the baby was born. She was in the room with me during my labor and everything.

Now as a grandma, she always takes him everywhere she goes. She treats him, exactly like he is her grandson and exactly the way he should be treated. I am very glad she does, too. My son is such a blessing. People always tell me, "You made the right decision." That makes feel good because everybody is agreeing with me now.

A few weeks later Monet's mother LaTanya was invited to give a talk at the annual Several Sources Shelters dinner. What follows is her very touching testimonial:

> Eight months ago, my sixteen-year-old daughter Monet's basketball coach brought

her home telling me she was pregnant. I went through a range of emotions. I felt like I had failed as a parent. I would teach her to wait until marriage to have sex. She was raised in a church to believe in God. This was such a disappointment to me. I was devastated. I was so upset and I was desperate. I made an appointment for my daughter to go to a clinic. When my daughter saw her baby's sonogram, she decided to keep her baby. As far as me, I had no connection to what she was looking at whatsoever. She was 24 or 25 weeks pregnant. That made me even angrier. So, I searched for a shelter for her. She was not going to live with me with a baby at sixteen years old. I found Several Sources. She moved in the very next day. As the days passed, my daughter would text me messages like, "With God all things are possible." She would say to me, "Mom, prayer changes things." And the last thing she would tell me, "If God can forgive me, I know you can."

Listening to my daughter softened my heart. I began to bring her home for the weekends. I was so grateful she had a loving and caring place to stay in an environment where she would be able to mature, and she also attended Ramsey High School. She was really mature and learning how to be a mom and that was really surprising to me.

Baby Gregory was born June 26, 2013, with his father and me by my daughter's side. Several Sources moms and housemothers came to visit her at the hospital. I felt like that was such a beautiful sisterhood and great community that they were able to show love for one another. They were able to give each other support through their struggles and their joys.

After the hospital, I stayed at the Prospect home a couple of days with my daughter. I wanted to help her out with Baby Gregory. But, I remember leaving and went home and remember crying, and I cried and cried, and I felt the emptiness inside, 'cause I had left my daughter behind. So I remember calling back to the house and my daughter was crying, too. She said, "Mom I want to come home." And I said, "Mo, I want you to come home, too." Eight days after Baby Gregory was born, my grandson and my daughter were back home.

Now, friends, I want to share something else with you. Twenty years ago, I was in a house fire. I had two sons that died in that house fire. They were two and three years old. So, I truly believe that this birth of Baby Gregory was God's way of healing my wounds. I truly believe that it was a blessing that he was born. She had a place where she could go to be able to save him so he could be born.

Monet is an excellent mother. She takes care and nurtures her baby. I think that God has helped her be peaceful and responsible. She is back at her regular high school and she is proud to be back on her basketball team. Funding for Several Sources is important because there are more babies and moms to be saved. They need all the help possible to provide a safe haven and continue their life-saving work.

Kathy, I want to thank you for your godly vision, and I don't know how to express our love for the work that you do. I want to thank you for opening up your home to provide my daughter with a nice place so you can nurture her. Not only did you save my grandbaby, you saved our family, so I just want to thank you all for listening and God bless.

What an amazing change of heart and mind. Just a few brief months ago a quick decision would have lost Gregory, Jr. forever. He would have been a distant memory. Kathy and all at the Several Sources Shelters join others in this country at this time to offer safety, hope, and the knowledge necessary to choose life for their preborn babies. This I have come to believe it truly what God wants and requires of us all. How could I have been so blind? I ask myself this question every time I pick up my grandson. If only I could hand him to you, I know you would see what I see and hear

> what I hear and feel in your hearts, and the love and mercy of God for us all coming from this innocent baby boy.
>
> I get it now. I thank God that I do. I got a second chance at life, not just for Gregory, Jr., but also for my daughter and for me. Thanks be to God and to the Several Sources Shelters and other organizations like them these precious miracle babies are saved and alive! I'm sure God is honored and more than pleased. I hope His faith in us must be renewed too.

I was there when Monet's mother came to pick her up at the shelter to take her back home. Monet's mother explained that when she returned to her house from leaving Monet and little Gregory at the shelter, her sense of loss was unbearable and she kept feeling something was missing. When Monet's mother returned only a few days after her grandson was born to pick up both Monet and Gregory, Jr., she stood up next to Monet and cried, saying to her daughter, "I'm not upset with you. I just need to apologize to you for not trusting you, for doubting you, and for making you feel ashamed or embarrassed, because I went through the same thing as a teenager. I want you to know that I love you and I'm always going to be there for you and my grandbaby and you don't ever have to leave unless you get married and move out.

"I really, really apologize for removing you from the house, but I think this was important. This had to happen. I had to work on my stuff for the months you were staying here at the shelter. I wanted you to have a beautiful pregnancy. I didn't want to damage your spirit. This was necessary. I love you and you're still my prize winner. That's why I came to get you and bring you home again. You got a mother and you got family and we're here to support you."

Monet remained quiet and humble. This sixteen-year-old had no feelings of anger, only expressed in her quiet presence as she held Gregory, Jr. a sense of forgiveness and joy that her family was coming back together.

A Meditation about Families

The Family of God is all of mankind. He is and shall be the protector and teacher of all of His children. Even as a child is comforted by holding the hand of his parent, so too must you be reassured throughout your life that God's Divine hand is outstretched to you. Reach out and take it. Walk with God. Talk to Him, for He loves you for you are His children. As His child, you must believe He will give unto you His knowledge and His help. As your children sat before you and were protected in your presence, so too must you know that God is always beside you. Call out for the Lord God, for if you have believed in Him, as you have lived these many years, you will know that He is still beside you now. And as you have kept the Lord unto your heart all these many

years, therefore, He shall hold you unto His Sacred Heart now.
All these things He shall do unto you if you but ask it of Him.
He shall forgive you your sins if you but ask it of Him.
He shall bestow His Love upon you if you but ask it of Him.
AMEN.

CHAPTER SEVEN

Everything's Going to Be Alright

In the scene when Apple's mother, June, comes to the shelter and desperately tries to get Apple to leave the shelter, and then Tom, Apple's father, arrives and is dismayed by all the confusion, Apple is traumatized.

At the shelters, emotions often run high. You can imagine with so many pregnant women how feelings are often in turmoil from the physiological changes to the dramatic shifts in their lives, their futures, and their relationships. I describe just a few in this book. Forgiveness is hard to find for those on the outside as well as on the inside of our Several Sources Shelters community. We must, therefore, work very hard to live by the words, "Forgive us our trespasses, as we forgive those who trespass against us." To be honest, every single chapter of this book could have these words included in the headings.

Margarita

Margarita was twenty-four years old and had known her friend for five years before dating him for five years. Here, she tells her story:

I knew my boyfriend since I was fourteen years old and now that I was twenty-four I thought I could depend on him; but, when I told him I was pregnant, his response was, "Get rid of it." Nineteen years ago, in January 1995, I came to Several Sources pregnant, alone, and very scared.

I made my decision. I knew his support was going to be none. I worked as long as I could, saved my money, and then contacted the Several Sources Shelters. I had no family in New Jersey. They all lived in Florida, Puerto Rico, and Cuba.

I was flipping thru the phone book and I saw a piece of the page with Several Sources Shelters on it and called the number. I kept in touch with them on a regular basis until January when I moved in and my son was born on March 3rd.

One of my favorite Several Sources memories was when Kathy was teaching a lesson on chastity and God's forgiveness of our sins. She brought christening gowns and each one had a black stain on it. Can you imagine? She said, "Just because you made that mistake, doesn't mean you'll be punished forever." She explained about Jesus' willing sacrifice on the Cross, which reopened the gates of Heaven. God therefore forgives us, as long as we promise Him that with His help, we are not going to sin again. She explained that God forgives you and looks beyond the black stain on your soul. He sees your inner beauty. He sees you as reborn.

I could move from my concerns about my relationship with God to my concerns about my baby. I was scared about my baby because I wondered how I could I love him because I had so much hatred in my heart for his father; but, fortunately, that went away as soon my son was born. His father never came to see him. My relationship simply ended at the beginning of my pregnancy.

As I listened to Margarita telling her story of betrayal, rejection, and ultimately the love she found with her newborn son, I remembered the love and acceptance Jesus showed the Samaritan woman at the well. He knew her sins and her broken heart. He offered her peace and comfort. As they talked at the well, Jesus ministered to the wounds of her heart and offered her an escape from her past. As was true with most people of that time, she had heard of a coming messiah, but did not understand fully what he would come to do. "The woman said, 'I know that Messiah' (called Christ) 'is coming. When he comes, he will explain everything to us.' Then Jesus declared, 'I, the one speaking to you—I am he.'" (John 4:25-26)

I think God gave me a sign when I needed it the most, something that renewed my faith not only in God but also in people. The first day when I had to come to Several Sources and I met Kathy, she took my hand and I felt like someone really cared about me. She touched my hand as she spoke to me, I felt so deeply moved. Somebody really cares! The compassion, the advice she gave me. When I think of my worst days I think of that one day and it helps me have a better understanding of people and I believe in the goodness of humanity again. When Kathy told me the title of the chapter featuring my story was going to be, "Everything is going to be alright," I remembered again this very special sign—this moment of peace and comfort she gave me when we first met.

The advice I would give other pregnant women is, first, value yourselves! This difficult time in your pregnancy shall soon pass. Keep God in your life and always remember that with Him anything is possible. You have to embrace the challenges of motherhood. Remember and have faith that God won't give you more than the two of you together can handle.

Also, you can be with someone more than ten years and not know that person. They can treat you like a fool and never show you their true selves. That's why I think I have learned the hard way that you should always be friends and not intertwine the physical with the emotional. If he really loves you, he would not have a problem waiting for you. Protect your heart at all times! You only have one and be ever so careful not to let it be broken by someone who is not worthy of your friendship and ultimately your love.

At one point in my life I did lose my way, but with God's help I got back on my feet and found the people and places I needed to get even closer to

Him. And the two ways I got closer to Him were humility and helping other people. I find such great joy in helping others. This I learned from all of you at the Several Sources Shelters. When my son was hungry, Several Sources never forgot us. The one-time packages would come every month with so many things, but what we seemed to need the most was the extra food gift certificates you always sent, and your love.

I had lost both my mother and my father just before I got pregnant. They were very old-fashioned about dating. I always had to have a chaperone with me. When they passed, I didn't have anyone in my immediate family, so God sent me my Several Sources family. These people have done for me what my own family couldn't have done, because they were not here physically to help me.

Recently, Kathy asked me to give a talk in a local church about what Several Sources Shelter means to me. That Sunday I had to give the same talk three times. Each time I gave the talk, I became more emotional because I realized over the past eighteen years I have grown as a person. I was crying tears of joy because I realized that I had grown mentally and spiritually. Several Sources was the one consistent thing in my life that I could depend upon. The people came up to me and said how brave I was and how they didn't realize the Several Sources Shelter existed and how it helps people.

When I called Kathy to share all this good news, I told her that I wanted to help again and again. My focus is to help her re-open the Several

Sources Shelter in Mendham. She is so worried and really wants to re-open this shelter before the Gimme Shelter *movie comes out because she knows pregnant women will be contacting her from all over the United States urgently needing a safe place to live.*

As she writes this book, we are trying to make plans for the Mendham shelter to open. I'm going to call local pastors in the area to see if they would let me come and speak just like I did this past weekend. Who knows? Maybe even as you read my words today, you'll decide to get involved. It would truly be an answer to many prayers of poor, suffering, pregnant women, abandoned and alone in this country who have nowhere to turn.

I have met many people in my life, but there is no one who is as selfless as Kathy. She lives, breathes, sleeps, walks, talks, and prays every moment of her life in service to God—asking Him to show her more ways to save babies by helping their mothers. She is infectious and I have happily and willfully caught the "bug." I have promised myself, Kathy, and (most important) God that I am going to do more to help women who suffered to have their babies as I did. My amazing son, Alden, is alive because of Several Sources and Kathy's determination to keep her shelter doors open. As of this moment, I have decided to join her baby-saving team. Alden is a freshman at Bergen Community College. He picked his major because he wants to "help people in need." Doesn't that sound exactly like what a Several Sources "saved" baby would say?

I used to take my Alden (the love of my life) on car rides, and sometimes we would drive past the Mendham Shelter. I'd explain to him, "That is where we lived when you were still inside me and that's the place that gave us a chance to be mother and son." I was blessed to have found my husband when Alden was six years old and he became the stepfather and male role model Alden needed. Now, Alden is just as determined to help Kathy reopen the Mendham Shelter as I am. Here are the speeches Alden and I gave at the Several Sources Fund Raiser in October of 2013. I hope you enjoy reading them as much as we enjoyed giving them.

Margarita: Hello, everyone. My name is Margarita. Nineteen years ago, I came to Several Sources pregnant—January 1995—alone and very scared. I found Several Sources in the yellow pages and met Kathy and then, through Kathy, I came to live at the Several Sources Mendham Shelter. I am so proud that I was invited here tonight. I have the honor to introduce my "baby." He is the love of my life. Alden, come and meet the benefactors of Several Sources Shelters.

Alden: The first thing I want to say to the benefactors is that my Mom is "the love of my life."

Thank you to all of you here tonight. Without you and your help, my Mom might

> not have been able to support me and take care of herself. When I was a baby, we lived in the Mendham Shelter and now my Mom and I were told, sadly, that due to lack of funds, the Mendham Shelter has been shut down. That's why we decided to come here tonight—to ask for your support to help Kathy reopen that Shelter.
>
> I want to tell you a little bit about myself. For the last eighteen years, Several Sources has never forgotten me and my Mom. They gave me school supplies, Christmas presents, and special holiday dinners. One of my favorite memories was going to the Christian Bible camp. You made a difference in my life and my Mom's life and I came here tonight to personally thank you for my life and I would also like to personally thank Kathy.

I think it is important for you to see the work not only as a supplement to the film Gimme Shelter but also as a tool to possibly start shelters in your own communities. This book explains the Several Sources Shelters journey—past, present, and future. You might wonder about our "future." My big question at sixty-six years old is which of these young women could possibly fill my shoes. Time will tell, but the important thing is that our "baby-saving" work must go on. No matter what the laws may be in our country or in our individual states, we will still need to help pregnant women who have nowhere to turn because of an unplanned pregnancy.

We must be careful not to nurture the seeds of hate as our young mothers may separate from their babies' fathers and loved ones who have let them down in their hours of need. The seed of hate is as a weed. It will spring forth rapidly and grow quickly with little or no assistance. And it will be difficult to uproot, for its roots will grow deep into the heart and mind of a person. The seed of love is fragile. It must be nurtured daily, for the weeds of the heart can surround it and they will try to choke the life from it.

Be one who plants into your garden the seeds of love. For in doing so you shall glorify the house of God. Tend to this garden, which will be in your heart and mind, nurturing it daily. If you do this each morning of each day throughout each year that you live, you swill bring glory to the Creator of all men and of all living things. For it is "A new command I give to you: Love one another. As I have loved you, so you must love one another. By this everyone will know that you are my disciples, if you love one another." (John 13: 34-35)

CHAPTER EIGHT

And That's Kathy with President Reagan

In *Gimme Shelter* Father McCarthy (played by James Earl Jones) shows Apple a photo of Kathy with President Ronald Reagan taken at the White House in the Oval Office. While Fr. McCarthy seems quite impressed, Apple seems not to recognize President Reagan.

In January of 1988, I came home from work to a message on my answering machine from the White House. Me, an average, everyday U.S. citizen actually getting a phone calls from the White House! I returned the call and found out I was invited to be an honoree at a ceremony at the White House hosted by President Ronald Reagan.

The story of my relationship with President Reagan goes back to 1984 when I was fined $10,000 by the state of New Jersey for running an unlicensed boarding house.

President Reagan played an important role in my life and in the destiny of the Several Sources

Shelters during the most critical time of our history and later when he honored our work.

As founder of Several Sources Shelters, I was housing unwed mothers at no charge by providing a place to live for three pregnant teenagers, a mother, and her infant son in my home. On August 2, 1984, the New Jersey State Department of Community Affairs said that I was running an illegal boarding house, notified me of an extensive list of sixty-five modifications I must make to my home and the $10,000 fine, which I mentioned earlier.

I decided to launch a campaign to oppose this order and wrote 138 letters to elected state officials in New Jersey as well as to President Ronald Reagan. After that, a White House staffer called me to say that they were, "hoping for a positive solution to the problem so that these young women and their children can have a good life." The White House saw what I "was doing as an act of Christian charity and no price tag could be put on love."

The staffer who did not want his name disclosed continued, "The White House is very sympathetic to the problem." He also said, "The President supports your program and is urging the state to allow you to continue operating." He then said, "You are to be applauded for the good work you have done. We will be in contact with the Governor's office with the hope that the best possible solution can be found so that the young women and children could have a good start in life."

On September 19, 1984, Carl Goldman, press secretary to New Jersey Governor Thomas H. Kean, made a statement that the Governor's office did receive a call from a White House official explaining, "They wanted to let us know that they are going to publicly support her."

I was extremely pleased; but, somehow, I knew this David-and-Goliath battle had only just begun and would take a long and difficult time to be resolved. Over time, other people had stepped forward to help other unwed mothers who needed shelter when my home had no open beds. Shortly after I was fined, inspectors visited two of these volunteer homes from the New Jersey Department of Community Affairs. The volunteers were told to complete a questionnaire about the relationships of the people living in their homes. They were told a search warrant would be obtained if they did not cooperate. We were all starting to get very frightened. They were coming down hard, which didn't make any sense to us.

On September 21, 1984, the official docket listed the case as *Kathleen DiFiore vs. the Bureau of Rooming and Boarding House Standards*; but, the local *Bergen Record* newspaper used this headline: "A Battle between Divine Will and State Will."

When asked by Administrative Law Judge Robert Glicken how I began my work, I explained that I had asked God for a direction in my life. I said, "I think I have a right to be a Christian. I think you are taking away my right to love God as I choose to."

The greater complication was the fact that even if I had made those sixty-five physical changes to my home, I still would have had to relocate because my residential home was not in a commercial zoning area, thus could not legally become a Boarding House. This became known in the media as "Kathy's Catch-22."

Two of the Several Sources Shelters teen mothers (Anna and Ann) came to the hearing with me for moral support. Taking the witness stand was intense and difficult. My future—and the futures of so many mothers and their babies—depended on the outcome of this case. I never knew what was going to be asked of me. I had a pro bono attorney, but the state came with two legal counsels, one of which was the State Attorney General, and several state officials to testify against me for taking in these young homeless pregnant women and their babies. As I sat in the witness chair being asked questions like, "Who cooks their meals?;" "Do you post weekly menus?;" "Do they pay you rent;" "Are there any rules, and, if so, how are they enforced?" My world and my faith-based work for these young mothers and their babies seemed to be slipping out of my control.

The courtroom was filled with reporters and camera crews. Every seat was taken and all my eyes could do was drift to the two young mothers who sat in the front row. They looked as frightened and concerned as I felt. But, one thing I remember to this day was a member of a TV crew, a young woman who sat on the floor holding a boom mike up to me. The strangest thing happened every time I look at her: a complete sense of peace would wash over me. The licensing requirement, the sixty-five modifications I would have to make to my home, the $10,000 fine, the Zoning Catch-22, the concern over what they would ask me next, and what our future would be—all of that seemed to subside when I looked at this young woman. I didn't know her name. I had never seen her before; but, when the trial was over, I just had to walk up to her and tell her about the experience. She smiled and quietly said, "I was praying for you." Never, ever doubt the power of prayer! If ever there was a day when I felt like it was me against the world, that was the day, except this young, faith-filled woman stayed there beside me and prayed. I think of her often and ask God to bless her for the spiritual support she gave me that lonely day.

I also remember one reporter who had visited my home in Ramsey several times with a local news crew. She simply asked, "How do you feel?" I tried to stay strong because I really didn't want to have the young mothers seeing me upset, but her words of compassion and sympathy broke me down. I just couldn't help myself. I remember crying as I explained, "I'm scared! I'm scared for the girls. I'm scared for their babies."

All the local media were covering the story including two wire services (UPI and AP). My most frequently asked question by the reporters was "Why do you do this?" I explained to them what I continue to say now, "I do this as a part of my desire to fulfill the gospel teachings and promises of Jesus. He said, ''Truly I tell you, whatever you did for one of the least of these brothers and sisters of mine, you did for me.'" (Matthew 25:40)

I explained that we're trying to help them to learn what life is like when you have God by your side helping and guiding you. It is important to us that the girls become better people. Some of the girls who come to me now have had no parenting. They come from broken homes. We share our beliefs and value system and let them feel the love of the Lord through us.

My Attorney argued, "*The Rooming and Boarding House Act* closes its eyes to the very essence of what Ms. DiFiore is doing. Legislature never intended the statute to go this far."

In October of 1985, I received a letter from the New Jersey State Attorney General explaining that Governor Kean would be vetoing the legislation. The reason stated was that, while my efforts for unwed mothers and babies was to be commended, the state had no way of knowing if other individuals would be as responsible.

That night, I watched the local news and saw Mother Teresa. She was with John Cardinal O'Connor in Manhattan on Christopher Street where she was opening an AIDS hospice. The Nobel Peace Prize winner was also in New York to address the General Assembly of the United Nations. I remember crying myself to sleep that night, praying and feeling I had nowhere else to turn as I laid my troubles at Jesus's Divine feet with a heart that lacked all hope.

When I woke the next morning and began saying my prayers, I thought I heard a small voice saying, "Contact Mother Teresa." I ignored the thought because I figured it was a product of seeing her on TV the night before.

Later, when I went downstairs to have some breakfast, I again heard the words, “Contact Mother Teresa,” only this time the words were so unbelievably loudly, I simply could not ignore them. I prostrated myself on the floor in awe and wonder (the first time I had ever done that in my life) and remembered that I had a business card from a man named Drew DeCoursey whom I had met earlier that year in Washington on the March for Life. Drew had told me that he often volunteered at one of Mother Theresa’s soup kitchens in New Jersey. When I called the number he gave me, Drew’s wife said that he had been with Mother Teresa the night before. She then gave me the phone number of Mother Teresa’s soup kitchen in Newark where Drew was. Drew contacted Sue Feeley, the head of New Jersey Co-Workers for Mother Teresa. Sue immediately called Mother Teresa in the Bronx and told her of my home, my work with unwed mothers and their babies. She explained my serious problems with the State of New Jersey. Mother Teresa kept asking Sue if I was a nun and Sue kept explaining that I was a private person who takes these young mothers and their babies into her own home. Mother Teresa offered to help me in any way necessary. She would personally visit the Governor, call the Governor, or write the Governor on my behalf.

Mother Teresa wrote a letter to Gov. Thomas Kean. In her letter, she urged the Governor to sign a bill allowing charitable shelters in private homes, stating:

> I beg you in the name of the little unborn children of New Jersey and their mothers not to veto the amendment to the Rooming and Boarding House Act.
>
> Jesus said, "Whatever you do to the least of my brothers you do it to Me." I beg you to help those families who are helping the Body of Christ and these unwed mothers and their children by taking them into their homes and by sharing their real love and concern.
>
> May God who is never outdone in generosity reward you with a great help that you can give to these needy people. Be sure of my prayers and prayers of my sisters for you.
>
> God Bless You,
> Mother Teresa

Fourteen days later, Governor Kean signed the amendment, which became law through the entire state of New Jersey.

A reporter asked me, "Who is your press agent?" I responded, "God!," for only He could have orchestrated the unbelievable series of events that happened in 1984 and 1985.

When I started Several Sources I did so by telling God that I was writing Him a blank check. He had access to everything I had and could use me

Darlisha's Certified Nursing Assistant diploma

Darlisha and Julian in Shelter Garden

Darlisha, Julian plus Wanda and Jordany were all in the film *Gimme Shelter*

Bill King on an outing with Newark children

Bill King with Cardinal O'Connor

Bill King visiting with women of Ladies Rest daytime shelter

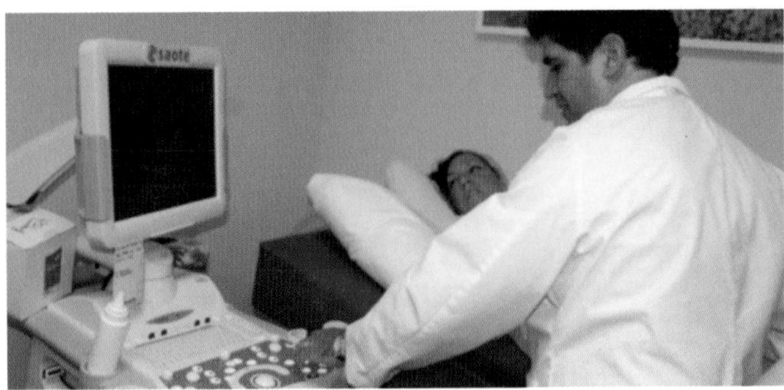

Erika at Our Gift of Hope Sonogram Center

Samantha's sonogram images

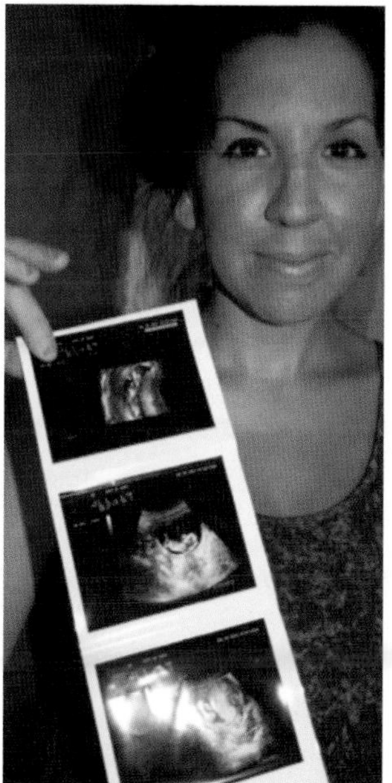
Erika's sonogram of her baby girl

Samantha's baby Noah

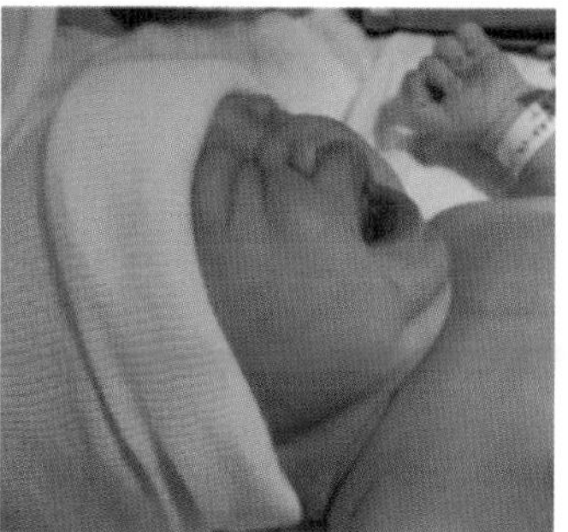
Erika's "saved" baby Faith born 1/19/14

Samantha with her son, Noah

Thalia with son Jonathan

Thalia with her sons, Jonathan and Brandon

Photo taken in 1989 of Kathy with 4 shelter babies including Christopher, second from left, and Liza on far right

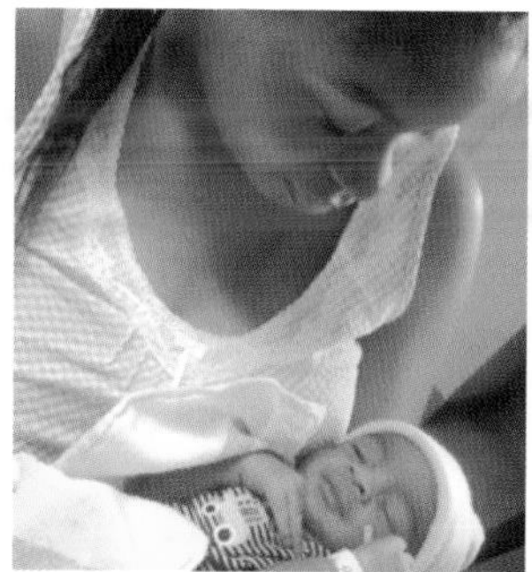
Monet with Gregory at the hospital

Kathy with Lana and Samantha at Christmas

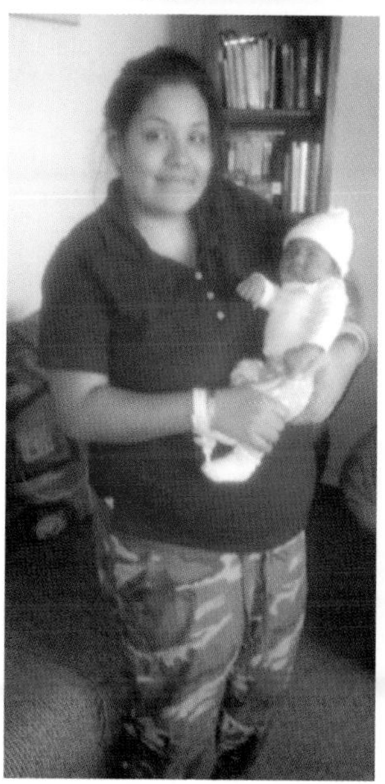
Lana and her daughter Liliana

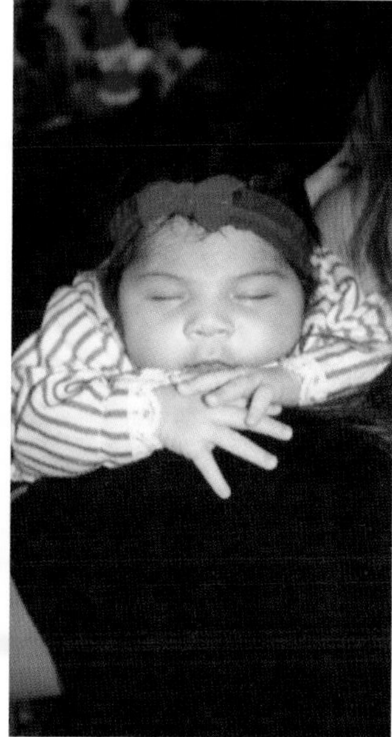
Lana holding Liliana on her First Christmas

Kathy with Margarita and her son, Alden

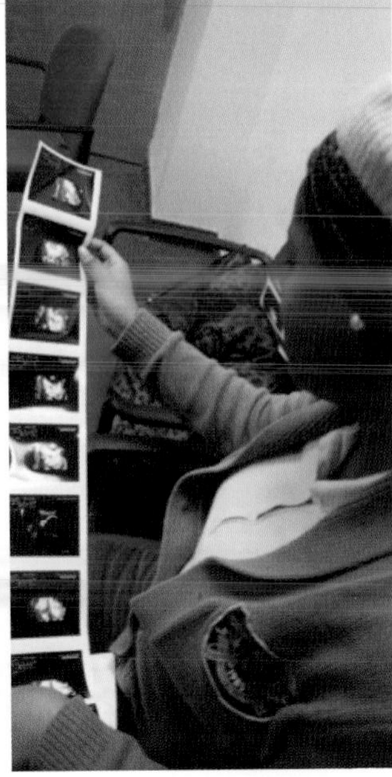

Monet receiving sonogram while Kathy observes

Monet's sonogram images

Kathy holding Gregory Jr. as Monet and Grandma beam with pride

Christopher with baby and priest

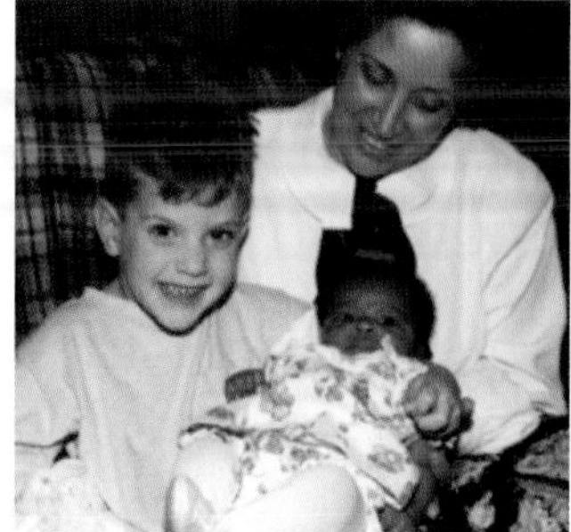

Kathy with Christopher and baby

The message of this statue of young Jesus in the Temple with no hands is, "We must become His hands."

Kathy with Archbishop Gerrity who referred Christopher's mom to Several Sources

Jimmy and his mom finding shelter from rough inner-city streets at Ladies Rest

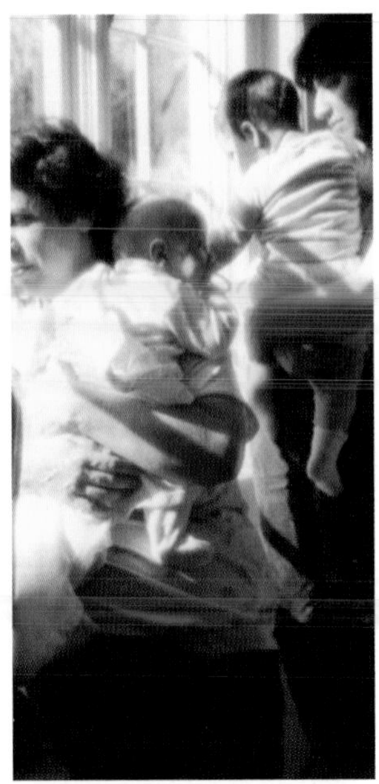

Linda and Christopher, Myrna and Liza

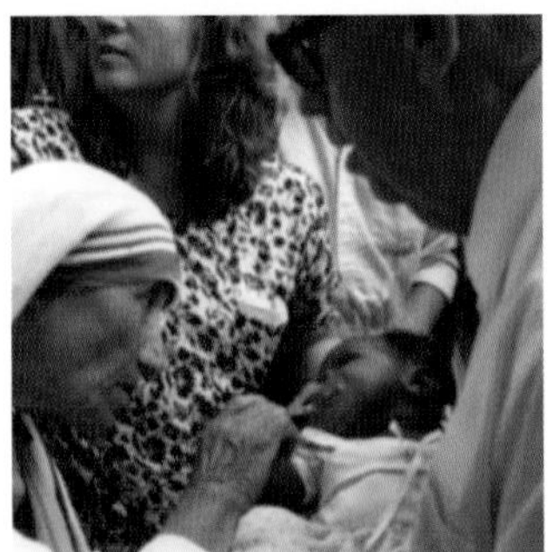

Mother Teresa blessing Toria's baby and thanking Richard Ryan for donating house

Kathy being honored by President Ronald Reagan at White House

Christopher speaking at 30th Anniversary Dinner

Liza's High School graduation

Kathy with President Reagan in the Oval Office

Myrna and Kathy with Liza at her graduation

His Holiness
Pope John Paul the Second
cordially imparts his special blessing
upon
Miss Katy Di Fiore

In 2014 Kathy received the Blessed john Paul II Gravitas Award for her efforts to communicate God's love through the film "Gimme Shelter".

THE WHITE HOUSE

WASHINGTON

February 18, 1988

Dear Kathy:

Thank you so very much for the framed photographs of some of the "Several Sources" children which you brought for me on the occasion of this year's March for Life and follow-up visit to the White House. I truly appreciate having this touching reminder of the inestimable value of human life. It's a perfect keepsake of the wonderful work that you and your fellow volunteers devote to the right to life movement.

Again, thank you -- and may God bless you always.

Sincerely,

Ronald Reagan

Ms. Kathy Difiore
Several Sources Foundation
Post Office Box 157
Ramsey, New Jersey 07446

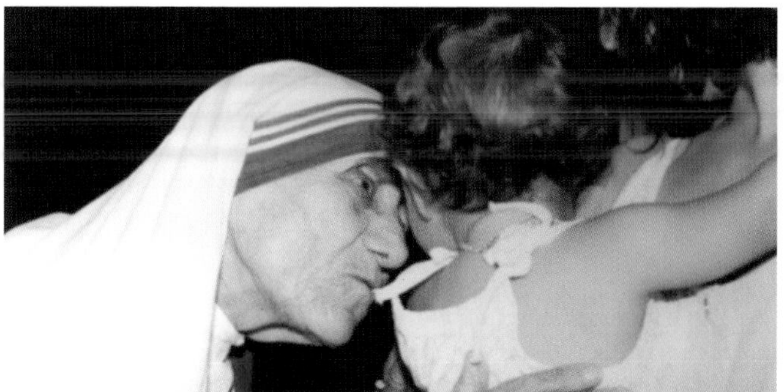

Liza meeting Mother Teresa during Several Sources visit in 1988

Kathy and Liza thanking Mother Teresa for helping to keep our shelters open

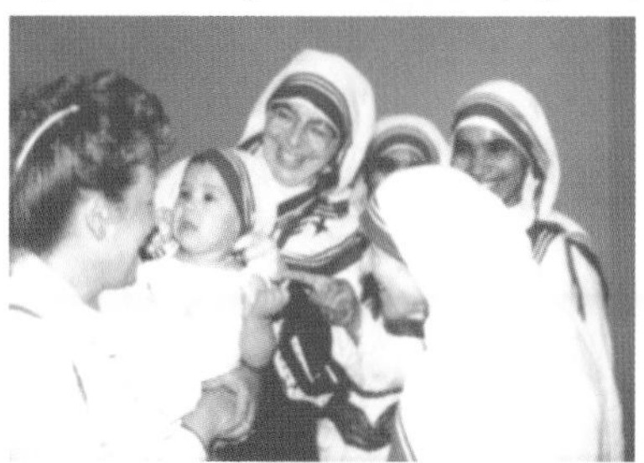

Mother Teresa and her Sisters enjoying a visit with Kathy and Liza

Myrna and Liza

+LDM

MISSIONARIES OF CHARITY
54A, A. J. C. BOSE ROAD
CALCUTTA 700016

9th December, 1988

Dear Kathy,

Thank you very much for your kind letter dated November 17th, 1988.

God's ways are so wonderful. He keeps using the poor to be His sunshine of love and compassion in the world by drawing us all together.

Keep up the good work you are doing. I pray that God may flood your soul with His spirit and life, so that you may radiate His love to all you meet.

God love you and bless you for the love you give and the joy you share through your gift to God's poor. Keep the joy of loving through sharing.

My prayer for you that you may grow more and more in the likeness of Christ through love and compassion and so become an instrument of peace.

God bless you
M. Teresa MC

MAKE US worthy, Lord to serve our fellow men throughout the world who live and die in poverty and hunger.
GIVE THEM, through our hands, this day their daily bread; and by our understanding love, give peace and joy.

God bless you
M. Teresa MC

LDM.

MISSIONARIES OF CHARITY
54A ACHARYA J. CHANDRA BOSE
CALCUTTA 700016, INDIA

13/1/90

Dear Kathy Defiore,

Thank you for your letter and your prayers for my health - I am much better thank you.

Keep up the good work you are doing - and remember whatever you do to the least you do it to Jesus - Do everything with Jesus, for Jesus Jesus, to Jesus through Mary - This way you will pray the work.

May God's blessing be with you & all those who work with you in 1990.

God bless you
M. Teresa MC

These are just 2 of the 6 letters Mother Teresa wrote for Kathy and Several Sources

Lizett and Erika viewing sonogram images at Our Gift of Hope

Lizett with Sidewalk counselors at Our Gift of Hope

Kathy with Maritza and Za'myiah

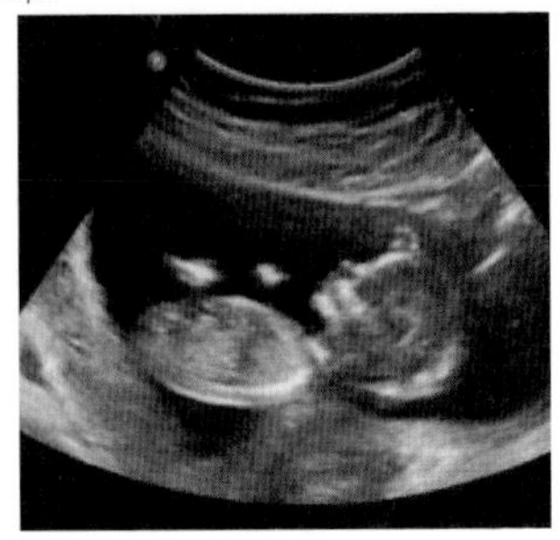

Sonogram of Lizett's daughter

Kathy welcoming Maritza to the shelter.

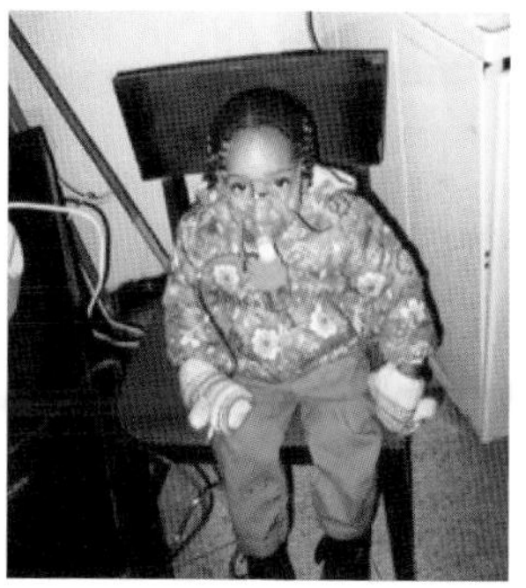

Jakiyah receiving Asthma medicine

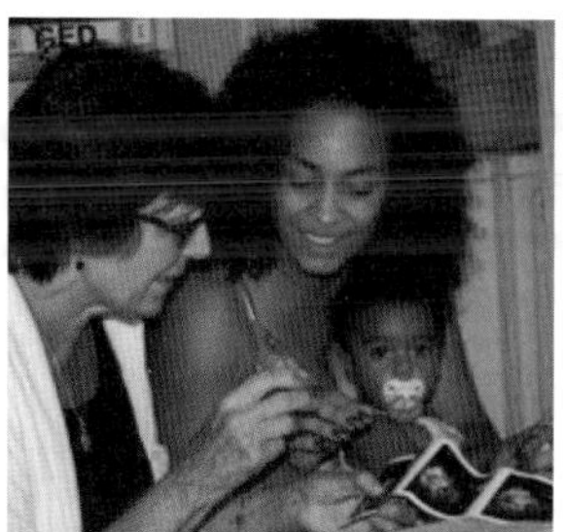

Maritza and Maureen looking at sonogram images

The Special Families at Bible Camp

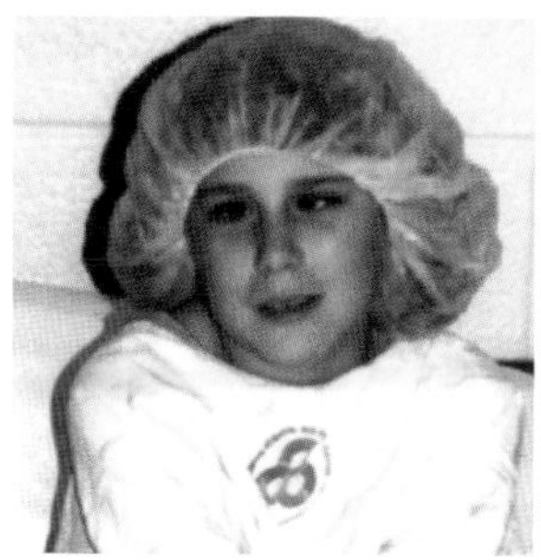

Betty receiving eye surgery

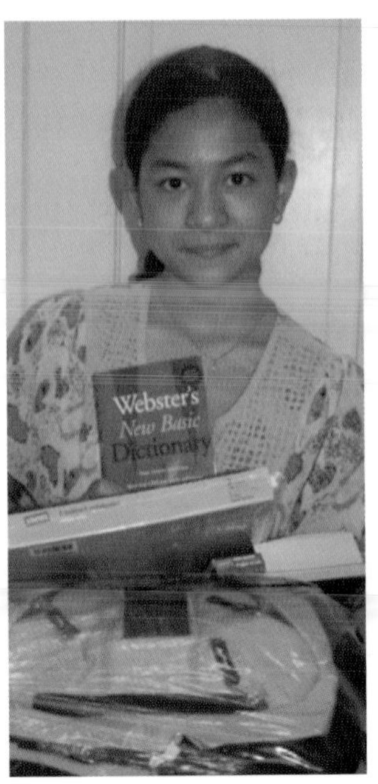

Special Families supplies delivered to Britney

Special Families supplies delivered to Brian

Special Famlies boy

Over 170 Special Family children receive school supplies every year

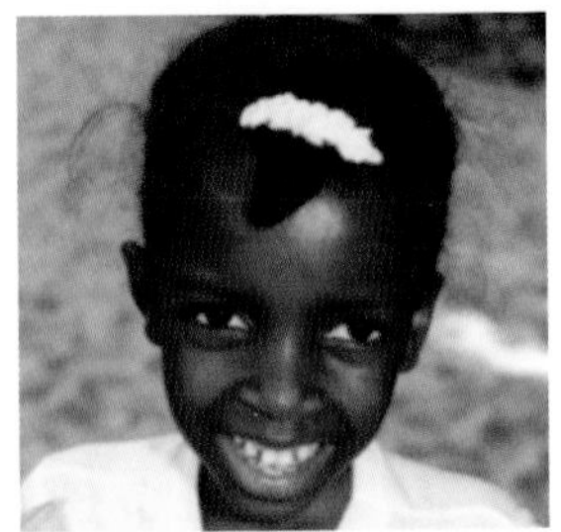

We helped Sarah's Grandma pay for her granddaughter's medical expenses

Michael at age 5

Michael graduates 8th grade

Michael's High School graduation photo

Special Families children enjoy a Summer picnic

Kathy with Phoebe, Special Families baby

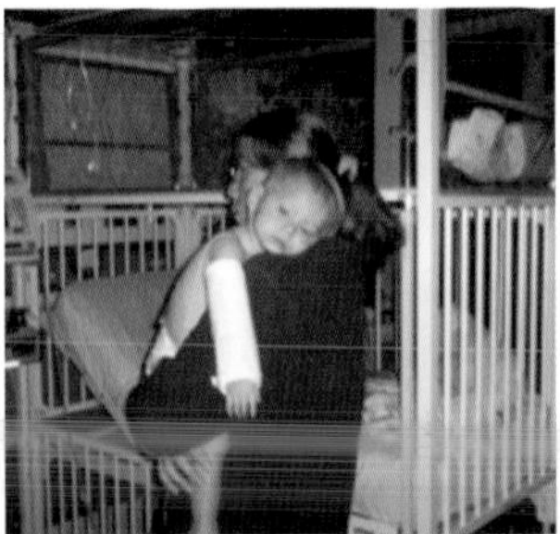

Ashley holding her daughter, Phoebe

Phoebe at 5 years old

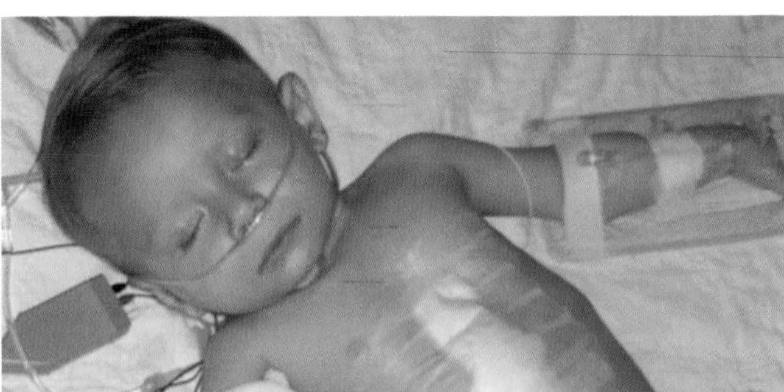

Phoebe after open-heart surgery

Christopher with woman at Ladies Rest

A homeless woman seeks shelter at Ladies Rest

Several Sources babies bring joy to Ladies Rest

Ladies Rest Manager, Charlotte, and the women of Ladies Rest are like a family

ST. PATRICK'S PRO-CATHEDRAL

November 19, 2013

Ms. Kathy DiFiore
Ladies Rest
74 Central Avenue
Newark, NJ 07102

Dear Kathy,

I just want to reaffirm how important your presence and mission at St. Patrick's Pro-Cathedral have been to us. Your work there in supporting women and guiding them in recovery from the devastation of their lives is truly an inspiration. I know that the focus on the dignity and blessing of the unborn child has been paramount in your efforts.

In the nice weather, I enjoy seeing the ladies relaxing outside and enjoying the refuge and safe shelter of "Ladies Rest". In the depth of winter, I am relieved to know that they found a warm and loving environment to get them through the day.

For the many years of your ministry in our midst, I am deeply grateful. Please know you and your wonderful staff are in my prayers and you have been a blessing in the life of St. Patrick's Pro-Cathedral.

Peace,

Rev Neil J Mahoney

Rev. Msgr. Neil J. Mahoney
Pastor

Missionaries of Charity Housemother, Pam and Charlotte

Msgr. Mahoney with Charlotte

Bible Study at Ladies Rest provides spiritual guidance to the homeless women of Newark

Unusual photo taken of the Ladies Rest crèche. Can you see the Dove?

Children wearing goggles we provided

Thank You signs from Ghana Quarry children

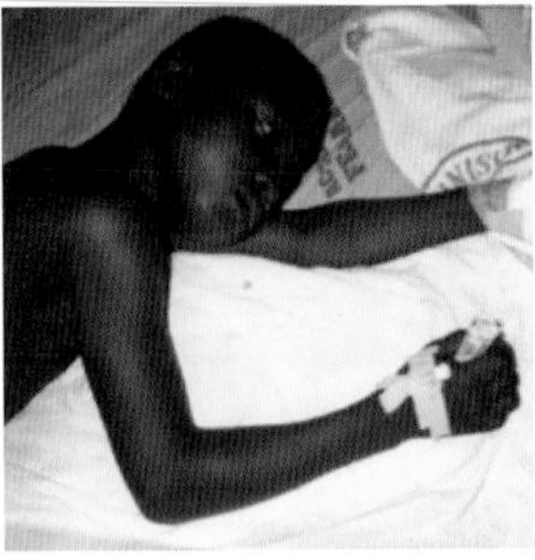

Ghana Quarry child after hand surgery

Ghana Quarry child working

Angela and Kyle from Our Gift of Hope - Ukraine

Tanya, Olga, Prim, and Katrina from Our Gift of Hope - Ukraine

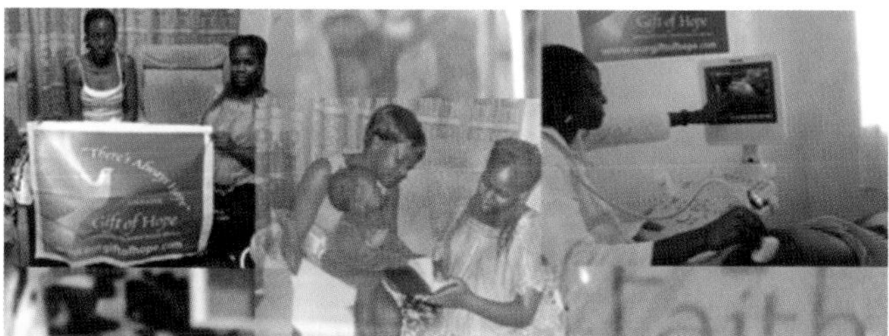

Gift of Hope - Uganda

Natasha, Malish, Prim, and Katrina from Our Gift of Hope - Ukraine

Kathy with kids from Chernobyl during visit to shelter

Kathy with boy from Chernobyl group

Girl from Chernobyl group

Kathy with Sergey from Chernobyl group

Kathy with Special Families member, "saved" baby Kathleen, with NY Cardinal Edward Egan

Party to celebrate Kathy's successful brain surgery

Kathy with Dr. Philip H. Gutin 3 days post op

Every year we take a photo like this at the shelter. One also appears in the last scene of the credits of the film ***Gimme Shelter***

Msgr. McCarthy holds "saved" babies Jordany & Avanna

Kathy's pet parrot, Rocky, bringing Joy to woman at Ladies Rest

Kathy with Julian, Emily and Emesha

Mothers and their babies celebrate Kathy's birthday. This photo is also in the film *Gimme Shelter*

Bible Study on Matt. 14: 22-23 Walking on water, Jesus says to Peter, "Why did you doubt?"

Kathy's first mothers and their babies (1981)

Kathy and Cardinal Timothy Dolan of New York

Katrina studying with Benjamin

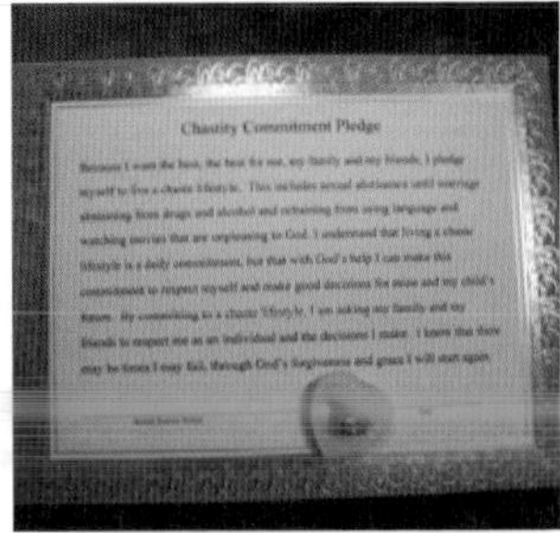

The Several Sources Chastity Pledge

Kathy speaking at church holding Ben

Kathy congratulating Several Sources mothers on their graduation

Kathy with Cardinal O'Connor

Painting Kathy commissioned to depict Bill King's meditation

CARDINAL'S OFFICE
1011 FIRST AVENUE
NEW YORK, NY 10022

December 16, 1988

Dear Kathy,

I have nothing but admiration for your magnificent efforts in helping young, some very young, mothers bring the babies in their wombs to birth, and then providing them and their babies with aftercare. As the President indicated, the pictures of God's little ones tell the story.

Words are inadequate to praise you and your volunteers. You can be certain that Our Lord loves you very, very much.

Faithfully in Christ,

John Cardinal O'Connor
Archbishop of New York

Ms. Kathy Di Fiore
Several Sources Foundation
P.O. Box 157
Ramsey, New Jersey 07446

THE ADVOCATE

The Newspaper of the Roman Catholic Archdiocese of Newark, New Jersey

VOL. 34 NO. 45 WEDNESDAY November 6, 1985 50 Cents

Will Kean OK homes for infants?

Mother Teresa of Calcutta has added her voice to those requesting that Governor Thomas Kean sign a bill which would allow private dwellings in New Jersey to give shelter to unwed mothers and their infants.

The bill, passed unanimously by both houses of the New Jersey Legislature, has been on the Governor's desk for more than a month now. He must act on it immediately after the Legislature resumes sessions on Nov. 14.

The bill was introduced by the late Sen. Garrett Hagedorn of Bergen County after Kathy DiFiore, who runs a shelter for unwed mothers in her Ramsey home, had been fined $10,000 for conducting "an illegal boarding home."

A spokesman for the Governor, after first denying that Mother Teresa's letter had been received, said that the Governor had no plans to respond to it, but would "take it into consideration when he gets around to making his decision."

Mother Teresa wrote the letter during her recent visit to the area to address the United Nations. It was then hand-delivered to Trenton.

Adolph Schimpf, president of the New Jersey Right to Life Committee, said "we are thrilled that this world-renowned humanitarian would take time out of her frantic schedule to join with the NJRLC and other pro-life groups to beg the Governor to sign this bill."

Schimpf also said that he was "shocked" that the Governor has to date "apparently ignored Mother Teresa's plea. He seems more interested in protecting his bureaucracy than in protecting the infants and their mothers."

No reason has been given for the delay in the signing of the bill. One suggestion is that the state bureaus which control boarding home operations have expressed concern that the bill would open the door for "abuses" of current regulations.

Parish workers are 'community'

"You are important because of your work in your parish," Sister Suzanne Golas, C.S.J.P., told those attending the Nov. 2 Essex County workshop for social concerns committees and peace teams at

Mother Teresa backs DiFiore

By JOHN BREUNIG

RAMSEY — Mother Teresa of Calcutta has joined Kathy DiFiore's battle to shelter unwed mothers and their babies in her Ramsey home.

The Nobel Peace Prize winner, who was in New York last week to address the General Assembly of the United Nations, wrote a letter to Gov. Thomas Kean urging him to sign a bill allowing charitable shelters in private homes.

"I beg you in the name of the little unborn children of New Jersey and their mothers not to veto the amendment to the Room and Boarding House Act," Mother Teresa wrote in the letter, according to Ms. DiFiore.

Local antiabortion agencies joined Ms. DiFiore last month when she picketed Kean's office to pressure him to sign the bill, which unanimously passed both houses of state legislature. According to Paul Walcott, Kean's assistant press secretary, Kean has not decided whether or not to support the bill and does not have to make a decision until the next Senate session, which is not yet scheduled but will not be held before Nov. 18.

"He is taking all the time he has before making a decision" Walcott said Friday. "He does support the concept of what she's (DiFiore) doing."

The bill, sponsored by the late state Sen. Garrett Hagedorn (R-Dist. 40), would allow private homeowners to house up to six unrelated persons. DiFiore was fined $10,000 last year for violating the Room and Boarding Act of 1979, which prohibits a homeowner to house more than one unrelated person at a time.

"When I was told Mother Teresa wrote the letter I got down on my knees and I thanked God," said Ms. DiFiore, who now houses three women and two children in her home. "To think that she knows that I exist is an honor. To think that she would take the time to help me and the girls is too beautiful to put into words."

Ms. DiFiore read a copy of Mother Teresa's letter by phone Friday.

"Jesus said, 'Whatever you do to the least of my brothers you do unto me.' I beg you to help those families who are helping the beauty Christ and the unwed mothers and their children by taking them into their homes and by sharing their real love and concern," Mother Teresa wrote in the second

See MOTHER TERESA, Page 3

Mother Teresa backs shelter of unwed

Newspaper article about Mother Teresa's support

State allows charity in home

FROM PAGE D-1

tions. So many people have helped," said Miss DiFiore, who is childless. She refers to the women she has taken in as "my girls."

"Quite honestly I have cried many tears wondering what would happen to my girls and their children," she said.

The new law permits the owners of single-family residences to take up to six people into their homes for charitable assistance. Owners are not permitted to ask the guests for money and are required to install smoke detectors.

"I'm just grateful the Lord has blessed us with this tiny little bill," Miss DiFiore said. "It's a beginning for girls who do not want to murder their babies and go through the brutal, traumatic experience of abortion. . . . I think if more people would open up their homes, there would be dramatically less abortions. A lot of girls who come to me have been forced out of their own homes."

State Sen. Gerald Cardinale, who advanced the bill after Hagedorn's death, yesterday went to Miss DiFiore's home to tell her the bill had been signed.

"We have Thanksgiving early," he said. The Demarest Republican also said he has been advised by aides to Kean that the governor would like to see more people undertake such charitable endeavors.

It was after her divorce in 1982 that Miss DiFiore decided to open

State makes charity legal

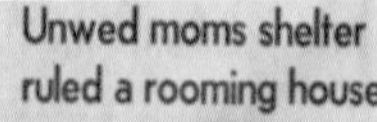

Unwed moms shelter ruled a rooming house

DiFiore meets Mother Teresa, Gov. Kean

Newspaper articles about Kathy's legal battle and settlement with the state of New Jersey

for whatever purpose He chose. This is my commitment to Him to this very day.

I love the job He has given me and sincerely hope He is pleased with what I am doing and how I go about the work He has assigned to me.

I have two little prayers I pray every day. One is "Dear Lord, help me set my priorities." And the other is what I like to call my "Two-by-Four" Prayer. I look at it this way: St. Joseph, Jesus' stepfather was a carpenter, and he taught Jesus to be a carpenter. So, there must be spiritual "wood" in Heaven. Since I have so much to do, and, at times I get distracted, I freely and willing ask Him to pick up a divine two-by-four and hit me over my head to get my attention to do His Divine will. I promised when He does so, I will immediately pay attention and respond to His request.

So, maybe the $10,000 fine was really a Divine "Two-by-Four." It was definitely God again, "writing straight with crooked lines" in my life. As long as He is pleased with me and the ultimate outcome, I'm just as Mother Teresa would say, "a pencil in His Hand."

How the invitation to visit President Ronald Reagan at The White House came about, I will never really know. I had been sheltering pregnant women in my home for seven years, but maybe the support President Reagan gave me in 1985 was part of the reason. The 1988 March for Life was planned to honor "everyday people" who were doing "everyday things" to help God's littlest ones—those who were still sleeping in their mother's wombs. Those of us who were invited were given strict instruction on what to do and how to do it. We were shown exactly how to shake hands with the President, when to smile, and when to turn our heads and look at the camera. We were also told not to say more than a brief "Hello, Mr. President." That was the protocol. So, one-by-one, the honored guests met President Reagan and had our photos taken both individually with him and as a group behind his desk in the Oval Office.

Then President Reagan addressed the group saying, "I am so appreciative of what you all are doing. We've been trying to get the Hyde Amendment passed and when we start talking about Constitutional Amendments, it recently struck me that actually if we really could get them to interpret things correctly, it's already in the Constitution, because these children are already human beings and are entitled to life, liberty, and the pursuit of happiness.

"I mentioned during my phone call this morning how twenty-four prestigious doctors in this country commented after listening to comments I had made, said that I was on very solid ground. These babies are human beings."

Again, we had been asked not to speak, but I was moved to say to President Reagan, "You are doing what our Founding Fathers did. You are bringing us back to God's values. That is what you are doing, and we thank you for that." Each of the other twelve visitors added their words of gratitude. Then, President Reagan stated, "I thank all of you. Continue to fight the good fight. God Bless all of you."

President Reagan seemed so very humble, almost embarrassed, and said, "Can we change the subject for a minute? I just can't resist knowing how you feel. I received a letter from a widow whose husband was killed in World War II and whose son is now in the military. She had this and sent it to me. You don't mind if I read it to you. This is the translation of a prayer found on a young Russian soldier, killed in action in 1944 whose name was Alexandr Zasipa."

> Hear me, Oh God. Never in my whole lifetime have I spoken to You, but just now I feel like sending You my greetings. You know from my childhood on, they always told me that You are not. I, like a fool, believed them. I've never contemplated your creation and yet tonight gazing up out of my shell hole, I marvel at the shimmering stars above me and suddenly know the cruelty of the lie.
>
> Will you, my God reach Your Hand out to me? I wonder. But, I will tell You and You will understand. Is it not strange that the Light should come upon me and I see You amid this night of Hell and there is nothing else that I have to say. This though, I am glad that I have learned to know You. At midnight, we are scheduled to attack, but You are looking on and I am not afraid.
>
> The signal...well, I guess I must be going. I have been happy with You. There is more I would like to say. As You well

know, the fighting will be cruel and even tonight, I may come knocking at Your door. Although I have not been a friend to You before, still will You let me enter even now if I do come? Why am I crying, oh my God, my Lord? You see what happens to me. Tonight my eyes were opened. Farewell, my God. I'm going and I am not likely to come back. Strange is it not, but death I fear no longer.

Then, President Reagan commented, "I wish I had that for Mr. Gorbachev when he was here. I thank all of you. Continue to fight the good fight. God Bless all of you."

How does one make the transition from such a powerful letter shared by the President of the United States to the specific story of another one of our Several Sources Shelter mothers and her son? The common denominator is the life-changing experiences that bring us closer to God—this soldier facing battle, the young mothers facing parenthood—all crooked lines that God uses to draw us closer to Him.

On December 16, 1988, I was blessed to receive a letter from John Cardinal O'Connor, the archbishop of New York, which mentioned my White House visit.

Dear Kathy,

I have nothing but admiration for your magnificent efforts in helping young, some

> very young, mothers bring their babies in their wombs to birth, and then providing them and their babies with aftercare. As the President indicated, the pictures of God's little ones tell the story. Words are inadequate to praise you and your volunteers. You can be certain that Our Lord loves you very, very much.
>
> Faithfully in Christ,
> John Cardinal O'Connor
> Archbishop of New York

Linda

Linda was working in St. Patrick Cathedral in Newark, New Jersey for Archbishop Peter Leo Gerety when she found out she was pregnant. She was thinking of "not having her baby," because she felt that she "didn't do the right thing in the first place" and that's how she got pregnant. She explains,

The Archbishop's Personal Secretary told me about Several Sources. Some people at the clinic had a kind of an intervention with me. They said, "Are you sure you want to do this? You might not ever become pregnant again."

I think God was doing this, not them. After they spoke to me, I left. I swear when I got outside, it was as if somebody was talking to me. I was standing there. I heard someone talking to me in my head. There was no one around me. I went back to

church and that's when the Archbishop's secretary gave me Several Sources' phone number.

When I made the decision to have my baby, Christopher's father didn't want to be around me anymore. I was thirty-nine years old and didn't want to carry a baby for nine months and give my child to someone else. I called the hotline and came for a visit and the next thing you know I was living with an elderly gentleman volunteer because Kathy didn't have any room at her house.

I cooked for him, and I think I spoiled him, too. Then Kathy finally had an open bed and I moved into her home. Living there was nice. I felt like a mother to the other girls because all of them were so young. After I had an emergency C-Section because his heart rate was going down, I told the doctor, "Don't you let my baby die. I don't care if I die. I want my baby to live." Chris was born on January 24, 1988. I had severe postpartum depression. The hospital brought a staff member to counsel me. I just didn't want to mother him. But then I saw his little face in the corner of his little carrier in the baby nursery. He was the biggest baby born that day at 9 lbs. 5 oz. I took one look at my son and said, "Oh, my God, he is so beautiful. I remembered all those Several Sources Bible Studies and I prayed saying, "Satan be gone! Just get out of here in Jesus' Name." Everything just fell into place, like a weight had been lifted off my shoulders when I just told him to get out of my life. I have God on my side now and from that point forward everything was good.

That was twenty-five years ago on January 24th, and that's the day of the release of the Gimme Shelter *movie. I was a first-time Several Sources mother at forty years of age, and my life changed a lot. I knew I wanted to be a good mother and I was going to make it.*

I was never close to God even though I worked in a church. The Bible studies helped me. Knowing that God sacrificed His Son's life for us touched me very deeply. I was a mother now and I just knew I could not do that. God is always there for us. He doesn't fault anybody. If you ask for forgiveness and promise to try not to sin again, He will forgive you.

Having Christopher made me grow up a lot. Kathy asked me to become a housemother and I agreed. I really tried to help all the younger mothers. Coaching them to keep on the straight and narrow wasn't always easy. I liked being on the hotline counseling pregnant women. I know what it was like when I was scared. The work was good and a blessing because I could help women to keep their babies. Several Sources helped me and I wanted to give back as much as I could and help other girls.

To this day, when women who Linda supervised call us, they will ask about her and tell us what a wonderful and loving mother substitute she was to them and, oh, how they loved the way she cooked! One thing pregnant women have in common is a great appreciation for good food.

Some of the girls had a hard time. The best thing was when they had to go to the hospital to deliver. Sometimes their families would come around and they would be reunited.

I really enjoyed when the young mothers and I were all together and talked about what we went through. We were like family getting together. I really liked it. I miss being around them. It brought a lot of joy to me and I just knew that we were going to be okay.

I was a housemother for nine years and the work was wonderful. Being a housemother is like being a second mom to the Several Sources mothers. I liked being there for the girls—showing them you care, getting them through things when they were having a hard time—was very fulfilling for me.

The most difficult part was having to leave because Chris was getting older and we had to be on our way. I think I would still be there if I could have stayed.

Kathy is the most kind-hearted person I have ever met. If it wasn't for her starting Several Sources and me finding out about it, I don't know where I would be today. It was like a miracle in itself. I learned a lot and I became a better person. It brought me closer to God and made me appreciate everything given to me that I would not have had if I hadn't found Several Sources. One of the other mothers, Myrna, who also became a housemother was my best friend there. She had her daughter Liza a few months after I had Christopher. We are still friends to this very day. Actually, she introduced me to my husband nine years ago. I said on our first date, "Sure hope you like kids because my fifteen-year-old son is part of the deal." Chris needed a male role model.

I think you might have to ask Christopher for what impact Several Sources has had on him. Chris didn't have a father as a child.

I would like to thank everybody at Several Sources for helping me and my son, Christopher. If it is wasn't for the benefactors there would be no Several Sources Shelters; if it wasn't for the benefactors and their generosity, I don't know where I would be today, so I thank you with all my heart. Even up to yesterday when Chris needed some very special medicine quickly I could call and get the help for him he needed. You guys are the best!

At our 30th Anniversary celebration Christopher who stands 6' 3" now, was a surprise speaker. He handed Kathy some beautiful roses and gave her a huge hug and began a short but very meaningful talk to all present.

> Hi. My name is Christopher and I'm twenty-two years old and I was a Several Sources "saved" baby. I just met a couple of the new "saved" babies that are living at Several Sources today—Viktor, Elijah, and Avanna. It's so good to see that Several Sources is doing as great as they are after thirty years being run by Kathy.

When I arrived here tonight, Kathy asked me what my earliest memory was of Several Sources. I said it was when we would go out to different homes and bring presents to needy children whose parents could not afford buying toys or anything for them. Just seeing the joy on their little faces at receiving our Christmas gifts was amazing.

Several Sources has done so much for me and my mom. I can't even explain in words how I am just so blessed, and how grateful we are to you guys. For Kathy, the benefactors, for anyone that has helped Several Sources, thank you. I am very blessed and thankful for everything you have done for us. Kathy, we thank you especially, for helping my mom and me. And we thank the benefactors for making this happen for the past thirty years. I hope all you guys keep doing what you are doing and have Several Sources go on for many more years to come. Thank you!"

Chris was so nervous but the applause helped to make him feel much better. To this very day comments are made about how wonderful his talk was and could he speak at other events. He's very shy. Maybe he will, but the truth is that every day of his life "speaks" to the gifts of life, hope, and love that come from Several Sources Shelters. Families are important to us all. For that reason I am sharing with you a talk I gave on December 19, 1984 four months after my battle with the state, I was invited to give a talk at the Elmwood Park, NJ Rotary Club. I choose the topic, "The Quality of Mercy in Our Lives. Is it Strained?"

> A young boy once asked his father this question, "Dad, if I were to become sick and die, would you be sad" Well, the boy's father was shocked at his son's question and asked him, "But son don't you realize that I love you very much? How could you doubt that I would miss you?" And the son replied, "How can I realize that you love me, if you have not told me?"
>
> How many of us here today have told our children that we love them within the last week? Within the last month? How many of us here have had our children say that they love us within the last year?
>
> Is the love between a child and its parents a quality of mercy? What is the definition of mercy? I define mercy as that quality which enables one person to relate to another with tenderness, with kindness, with love, and with understanding toward another.
>
> I will not preach or lecture others as to how they should raise their children, for surely you as parents know your children and are

best suited to raise them; but, I will speak of other children that I do know of.

These children are those young girls who have come to live at my house in Ramsey. These young girls found themselves pregnant and unwed. Most of them were thrown out of their homes by their parents, so I took them in.

Several other families also took them into their homes. They fed and sheltered them until they could have their babies; they gave them love and understanding; they helped them.

We at Several Sources do not condone pre-marital sex. We do not encourage young women to become pregnant. But, as a charitable organization, we feel compelled to help these women who have no other place nor person to turn to. Many of these girls' parents have told their daughters to terminate their pregnancies. Unfortunately, in many cases these young girls have been forced against their wills to do so.

Several Sources Shelters does not support ending pregnancies; therefore, we house these young girls until they have their babies and hopefully they can even return to their families or perhaps even marry the father of the child. I have observed in speaking to many of these girls that they have felt unloved at home. Perhaps this has lead them to seek love elsewhere. I cannot say for sure, but that possibility exists. Many of the girls have told me that while staying with me at my home that this is the first time they have felt part of a family.

I would like to ask each of you to think of this: How is your child to know that you love them unless you tell them? And if you are not to tell them, shall they seek love elsewhere? Several Sources is a last resort for unwed mothers. But should not their own home and their own parents been the first resort? The girls I house are not "bad." Most are very confused. Some are very juvenile in their behavior; but, by and large, they are sincere. I would like to leave you with this thought. I do not doubt that you do love your children; but, sometimes children, being children, interpret disciple for lack of love. They interpret a parent being absent from home as a lack of love.

Several Sources was founded to help people. One of our most important goals was to help unwed mothers; but, in truth, I must say I feel this should be the responsibility of the parents, for these are their children. Who better knows a child than its parents? Who better can supply the love and understanding than the child's parents? We will continue of course to help these children. But I hope that someday it should not be necessary for us to be surrogate parents. Ask yourself: "Is the quality of mercy strained between myself and my child?"

CHAPTER NINE

That's Kathy with Mother Teresa

In *Gimme Shelter* when Fr. Frank first comes to the Several Sources Shelters with Apple, he shows her a photo of Kathy with Mother Teresa. Apple seems to listen but not understand. She did not comprehend that her sixteen years of difficult living, much of it on the streets suffering and being abused, made her exactly the type of person Mother Teresa would have wanted to befriend and help.

The day we were invited to meet with Mother Teresa at the Sacred Heart Church in the Bronx, NY during the First Profession of Vows of Brothers in her order, the Missionaries of Charity, turned out to be a day filled with miracles and unexpected blessings. Three of the unwed mothers and some of our Several Sources volunteers came with me. We were all tired, but full of joy and amazement while the mothers listened intently, as one-by-one, they shared their personal anecdotes about Mother Teresa.

Laurie was twenty-one years old and expecting her baby in November of that year. Laurie told me, "All through school, we used to get books and magazines about Mother Teresa, but to actually meet her was so exciting. As I went through the line, people were pushing and everything. It made me very nervous. She wasn't an everyday Nun! As I approached her, I gave her a kiss on the top of the head. She looked up at me with such compassion in her eyes. I could actually feel her looking through me. She clutched my hand and then said something, but I couldn't make it out. She put her hand on my tummy and blessed the baby. I felt different—happier, peaceful, knowing that everything is going to work out just fine."

Carol was nineteen and her baby was one week overdue. Carol's parents did not agree with her having a baby and she was quite scared and didn't know what to do until she found the Several Sources Shelter. Now, she was standing before the one person in the world who everyone agreed was a Living Saint. Carol shared, "As I got closer to her a warmth overpowered me. As I stood in line waiting for my turn the first thing that hit me was, 'Wow, she is really short!' Then it was my turn. It was as if I was meeting an old friend or relative. I was just so calm.

"The first thing she did was to look into my eyes and smile. I said, 'Hi' and was about to walk away, as everyone else had done, when suddenly, she grabbed my hand and pulled me back. She looked right into my eyes and said something as though it was to be a secret between both of us and

God. Then, she slowly moved her eyes down toward my stomach. Releasing my hand, she started to pat my stomach. One of the priests gave me a medal, but Mother Teresa held my hand again and said, 'Give, for the baby. Give more for the baby.' And so I ended up with 4 medals. For some reason, I had a feeling of being watched, not only by the crowd, but by her and by God. And for me, that's a feeling that will never subside."

Suzette was nineteen and originally from Trinidad. Her little daughter, Katurah, was born only six weeks prior. Suzette explained, "Meeting Mother Teresa was like a dream for me. I never thought for one minute I would be able to reach out and touch this blessed lady, but I did. Mother Teresa touched my hands and said to me, 'God bless you.' Then she put her hand on my daughter and blessed her. That was one of the best things that could ever happen to little Katurah. Someday, when she can understand, my daughter will see the picture of Mother Teresa blessing her. She's going to treasure that picture for the rest of her life. I think that Katurah and I will have a memory that will always be cherished between a mother and a daughter."

Then my turn came to meet Mother Teresa. When I introduced myself to Mother Teresa, she smiled and said, "May our dear Lord bless you for always being available to Him to help the poorest of the poor—the unborn children." Then she turned to someone who was assisting her and asked for three Miraculous Medals and placed them in the palm of my hand, one at a time, saying, “One for the Father, one for the Son, and one for the Holy Ghost.”

I was so stunned because I always spoke of the Holy Trinity. I’ll never forget that moment. I tried to thank her for all the help she had given us to keep our shelters open, but I can’t be sure she understood what I was saying. She did say, “God’s ways are wonderful. Keep up the good work you are doing for the mothers and their babies. This work is most important to Him. The Sisters and I will be praying for you and for all who work with you so that you radiate God’s love to all you meet.”

As I explained earlier, when the New Jersey State Senate and Assembly responded by unanimously passing legislation that would exempt homes like mine from the law, my efforts to help the pregnant women seemed doomed by bureaucratic red tape and the possibility that the Governor might veto the bill.

Mother Teresa was in New York to open a home for AIDS patients. I contacted her and she decided to become involved in my plight. That is when she wrote a letter to Gov. Thomas Kean, pleading with him to sign the legislation, which would legally permit people to house the unborn and their mothers.

Fourteen days later, on November 14, 1985, the amendment became law. Since that time, the blessings continue to flow. In September 1986, Richard Ryan, of North Plainfield, NJ donated his New Jersey Shore vacation home to the Several Sources Shelters, which has helped to save five babies, including one set of twins.

Richard brought one of the "little ones" up to Mother Teresa, who, after blessing the baby in his arms, said to him, "I must bless you, too. Isn't that wonderful? So many girls need help these days. It is wonderful to hear of someone helping to save babies by giving houses."

Tired from the day, Mr. Ryan sat in my living room and said, "Mother Teresa seemed to be full of joy when she heard about the house in Sea Isle City. I've always felt that if we could provide a safe place for these girls, they would come there to have their babies."

During a two-hour ceremony in the Bronx, Mother Teresa spoke of the unborn:

> When Mary went to visit her cousin, Elizabeth, something very strange happened. When she came, the little one, the little child in the womb of his mother, Elizabeth, leapt with joy. How strange that God should use an unborn child to proclaim the coming of Christ. And we know that a terrible thing is happening today to that unborn child that the mother would kill the little unborn child in her own womb. That is why we must thank God for the great gift of these two Brothers that he has given us.
>
> These Brothers have consecrated their lives to Jesus. Thank their parents for giving them life, for giving them love, for giving them the joy of living, the joy of loving one another. Let us thank God for our own

parents, who wanted us, who gave us the joy of living and pray for the parents, all parents, that they will love their children. Love their children thru the grace of God's Son, the Lamb of God. We are Jesus' family. He came to give us the good news that God is love; that He loves us; that He wants us to love one another; that He loves each one of us.

And to make it easier to love one another, He said something very difficult. "Whatever you do to the least of My brothers, you do for Me. If you give a glass of water in My Name, you give it to Me. If you receive a child in my Name, you receive Me. For that little one that He created is the greatest gift of His love; His spirit; made in the image of God."

God wants us to love one another as Jesus loved you and the fruit of love will be to increase our faith. And I will pray for you that you will love one another and grow in holiness. Holiness is only a simple duty. It is a simple duty for which God calls us and where there is love there is peace. Pray that the peace of God will come to us daily and the fruit of love will be a deepening of faith. And the fruit of faith is love and the fruit of love is service and the fruit of service is peace. That is why we must pray

> especially when we serve. We must pray to Our Lady in a special way.
>
> So let us ask Our Lady especially to pray for our families and to give us the joy of giving the greatest gift of all—of loving one another with God's love.

The day ended with each of us feeling filled with the grace of the Holy Spirit and a desire to serve God in our individual ways. Mother Theresa showed us God's infinite patience, understanding, and love. All four feet -seven inches of her just beamed His Presence. Our "baby-saving" work has continued with the goal of always trying to follow in Mother Teresa's footsteps. After all, if it weren't for her, our shelters would not have remained open.

Mother Teresa's Christ-like example and her involvement as our champion—writing the New Jersey Governor, begging him to keep our home for mothers and their babies open—were gifts we could never have imagined. There is one other treasured gift from her Missionaries of Charity we were blessed to receive. They were replacing a very old crucifix from their chapel in Newark and gave it to us for our main shelter where we conduct our bible studies and chastity workshops. Jesus' eyes and mouth are open as He is depicted saying some of his last words to Our Heavenly Father. Mother Teresa proposed they were "I thirst," suggesting He thirsts for souls. I often wonder, particularly in these complex, confusing, and dangerous times, if He is not saying, “Forgive them Father, for they know not what they do.”

In January of 1989, Sister Kathleen [Missionaries of Charity Superior of the Newark shelter] reached out to me about the possibility of her referring pregnant women to the Several Sources Shelters. The Sisters were operating a nighttime shelter there and sometimes a pregnant woman would need housing. I told Sr. Kathleen we would most definitely help and also would like to come with some of our current mothers and babies to visit her, the other sisters, and the women of Mother Teresa's shelter called “Queen of Peace Shelter” on Jay St. Sr. Kathleen agreed, and soon we had created a relationship to help one another.

“I don’t feel that I’m doing enough to help others in this world,” sighed Myrna, an unwed mother at the Ramsey Several Sources Shelter, as she packed the station wagon with gifts and food for a trip to the Missionaries of Charity in their Newark shelter and soup kitchen.

Myrna, along with seven other unwed mothers, adopted the Missionaries of Charity as their sisters. The mothers felt they were blessed and their hearts were touched by the kindness and charity shown to them by the parishioners of New Jersey churches. This motivated the mothers to reach out and share their blessings with those less fortunate.

“At least we have a roof over our head each night,” said Toria, a sixteen-year-old at Several Sources, “and we know where our next meal is coming from.”

To this day, we make several trips to the Missionaries of Charity women's shelter and soup kitchen during the Holiday Season. We take toys for homeless children and gifts of clothing and food for their families.

The Newark shelter houses twenty women and feeds more than 200 men in their soup kitchen each day. Linda, one of our former housemothers, enjoyed cooking for the homeless ladies. She explained,

It was just something I could do to help the homeless ladies feel a little better about their lives. It made them happy. My heart went out to them because they had so little to share compared to us. Even though we lived in a shelter, they had it worse because they had to go out in the cold during the day and we didn't. They really loved to see our babies. I think Christopher liked being with them too. He never cried or fussed when they held him.

They were a blessing to us all. It was a way to give back considering all that we were being given. It was just special. It felt like we were doing God's work. Mother Teresa, the Sisters, and the co-workers have been a spiritual inspiration to our unwed mothers. Each time that we visit and help them we take home the spiritual blessing that comes to those who help their fellow man.

Several New Jersey church groups have donated toys and baby clothes to the Several Sources mothers during the holiday season. It was the girls' idea that these gifts be shared with the homeless babies and mothers at the Newark

Missionaries of Charity shelter. On their first visit, the Day Room looked so bleak that we decided to erect a Christmas Tree to cheer things up. The homeless children and mothers helped to decorate the tree.

"No one, not even the poor should be without a tree at Christmas time," Myrna said. "You should have seen the faces of the children light up as the lights on the tree were turned on."

Myrna

Myrna's stay with Kathy was unique because at the time Myrna came to live with Kathy, Several Sources had only the shelter in Kathy's home. Myrna shares,

What I remember most about my pregnancy was the need for a place to live and how important it was for me to stand my ground to give life to my child

I was working and going to college when I found out I was pregnant. No one understood why I wouldn't just quietly "get rid of the problem," and why I would risk my future with the responsibility of raising a child. But, I already had lost my first child to a poor decision and knew I couldn't go down the road again. My life hadn't really gotten any better because I made that sad choice—only worse—and here I was in the same situation again. I had to do something different. I had to trust that God was true in his promise to never leave me or forsake me (Hebrews 13:5). That life was good and God is good, (Psalm 100:5) and life is his gift. He carefully creates and forms each one of us in the womb

(Psalm 139 13-16). I stuck by my decision and it cost me. My family didn't understand. My mom didn't want me to tell my grandparents. At six months, I finally went to visit them with the news and got mixed emotions from them.

Everyone saw this as a problem to be solved by a simple procedure and I could go on with my so-called life without my baby. I couldn't find an apartment after my lease was up. It seems renting to a single mom was too risky to the landlords I met. I ended up completely homeless. But I was strong on the inside. I knew I was doing the right thing before God. The Bible says, "There is no fear in love but perfect love casts out fear." 1 (John 4:18) I believe that is why I could get through all the stress and uncertainty, because my spirit remained strong

My decision to have my baby made it difficult for others to help. Even my own parents found it impossible to have me in their homes knowing that soon there would be a new life to care for. I was so desperate for help. After months of struggle I had a Bible and asked God to help me. Opening to John 14, I read, "In my Father's house there are many rooms." It was as if he were telling me that there was a place with room for me. I opened the phone book to look for a shelter and found a shelter, but they had no openings. They referred me to Kathy's home. After an interview with Kathy, I was accepted into her home and went to live there. I was at peace!

Finally Liza was born! Liza's birth was "a party." My dad was with me in the delivery room, all my brothers and sisters visited. It was so great after so much stress to get to that point to see everyone so excited that she was born. And what a gift her life is to so many!!! Liza is a cheerful happy, positive woman. She has always been this way. Her life is a victory and I believe she lives that victory every day. Her first year of life was a celebration of life of what God can do through others and a celebration that the future was bright for us. "The steps of a righteous man are ordered by The Lord" (Psalm 37:23). You don't have to worry about your future. God will guide you.

I decided to become a Several Sources housemother because I wanted to help other women in their journey. To be a family to those who had to forsake many times their own family and friends so they could have their children. I believed God gave me a great gift when He allowed me to serve Him and His people in this way.

What I loved best about being a housemother was sharing: conversations, experiences, tips on mothering, heartbreaks, and triumphs. It was a very special time in my life, and for my daughter. I grew in so many ways, especially sharing with women on the hotline who were so frightened and confused, lacking a support system at home. I tried to give women a glimmer of hope—the acceptance they were looking for when all they really wanted to do was have their babies in peace—while others were wearing them down with horror stories and threats of what might happen if they chose to have their babies.

Several Sources is a cherished place in my heart. I can never fully explain what those years meant to me and how they changed my life. I believe that the love and hope I received there have made me the woman I am today and have directly impacted my husband, my marriage, and my children for the best. When you apply God's words to your own life, they will overflow into every area of your life. We are happy, we are blessed, we are together and we have the Lord. I can't ask for more!!!!

When I look at my kids today, I am grateful that I didn't fall into an worldly mindset that says we can we can eliminate and extinguish a life if it seems to get in our way. One time was one time too many and, as I see my four kids, ages 13 to 25, I smile. They have each other; they love each other. What they have, no one can take from them—they know and love God. It's the greatest gift of all.

One of the single most exciting things that happened to Liza and me when we were at Several Sources was when Kathy told me that we were going to get a chance to meet Mother Teresa. The night before I was going to see her, I just couldn't sleep. I was so excited that morning. I kept wondering, "Would I get to talk to her. Would I get to touch her?" Then we got in the van and the next thing I know she was there before me asking me two questions, which I will never forget.

First she looked at Liza and asked, "Did the baby eat today?" I was so surprised. She was concerned about my baby. I immediately said yes, and then she surprised me again and asked, "Did you eat today?" She was concerned about us! And she was so filled with joy. I got to see a living saint—someone who lived out their faith. She lived what she truly believed—that it was possible to live a holy and devoted life in this world.

My twenty-five-year-old daughter, Liza, talks about that day all the time. She'll say, "A saint touched me and wanted to know if I was okay!"

Kathy shares devotional books with us all the time. One of my favorites is Eileen Egan's book Such a Vision of the Street: Mother Teresa—The Spirit and the Work *that she gave me with this inscription,*

Dear Myrna,

Together let us journey through this book and be inspired by the holy works of this Blessed Mother Teresa. Let us pray that God's most Holy Spirit will help us to accomplish the task He has given us. May Mother Teresa's life as a Missionary of Charity help us to find the wisdom strength and patience we need to become and remain God's "Missionaries for life."

Your Sister in Christ,
Kathy

We have Mother Teresa's picture with Liza, Kathy, and me in our house as a cornerstone of how we want to live our lives. To see her love in action helped my love for God to grow into unconditional love for everyone in general, and for my family in particular.

I've had a lot of time to think about it. My daughter is now twenty-five and that time with Mother Teresa has impacted both of our walks with God. This part of my life's journey made Him more real. I was just coming into my faith. It was something my daughter and I shared, and it is part of our family history. My husband talks about it constantly. Nothing trumps meeting Mother Teresa: no queen, no king, no president.

There is joy in serving the Lord. That's what I saw in her that day. Her eyes were glowing. Her personality was bright. She was in tune with me. "The joy of the Lord is my strength and Shield" (Psalm 28:7). I would think of this psalm often when I think of Mother Teresa. In that way I feel like I still have a connection to Kathy and I can learn from her every time I read about her or her words and philosophy.

Liza also shares her thoughts on Mother Teresa, *When I look at the photos of me with Mother Teresa I feel blessed. I was only a baby and that makes it more special because I was able to touch someone as holy as her. . I wonder at times did a part of her has rub off on me. Every time I look at those photos of her with me, I feel warm, happy, and peaceful. I have read books about her often. Then I go back and read them again, just to get a better idea of how she lived her life and what she thought. She really is someone I look up to a lot. I guess part of that is because both my mother and I got to meet her.*

There is a quote of hers that I really like about helping people, "Let us not be satisfied with just giving. Money is not enough, money can be got, but they need your hearts to love them. So, spread your love everywhere you go."[8]

She has had an impact on my whole family. She pushed us in the right direction. She gave us a sense of peace and hope. Most of all she helped to change the law in New Jersey, so she could keep Kathy's house running so my mother and I had a safe place to live. Even my little brother understands that she is very special. I'm so grateful that she was able to help out the shelter. I think that's wonderful that someone should be so caring and wonderful about that. She was always caring and always giving. She was full of love and life. To this day, I wonder how that holy experience affected the person I have become.

One of my first letters from Mother Teresa dated December 9, 1988 was from Calcutta and in it she writes,

> Dear Kathy DiFiore,
>
> God love you and bless you for the love you give and the joy you share through you gift to God's poor. Keep the joy of loving through sharing.

The gift of God's joy from doing His work was so important that Mother Teresa emphasized the word twice in one sentence. I believe she was trying to share with me, you, and the world that the

8. http://www.brainyquote.com/quotes/quotes/m/mothertere153714.html

love God has for all His children is a blessing to be enjoyed and shared. Again and again, she wanted to teach us to enjoy the work God brings into our lives. We are just so very blessed that she shared her joys and her understanding of the need to be joy-filled with us, as we attempt to walk with Him every hour of the day.

What do you think was one of the most joy-filled moments Jesus experienced? I think it may have been when he was surrounded by the little children:

> Then people brought little children to Jesus for him to place his hands on them and pray for them. But the disciples rebuked them. Jesus said, "Let the little children come to me, and do not hinder them, for the kingdom of heaven belongs to such as these."
>
> —Matthew 19:13-14

Imagine what that scene looked like: full of joy, full of life, sharing good will, and the smiling faces of all the children, their parents, and most of all Jesus, the Christ. And He shares with us an important teaching that "Heaven belongs to such as these."

Mother Teresa knew how to share joy at the most unusual time and in the most unusual places. Once Sr. Kathleen called me saying that Mother Teresa was in Newark to visit an old friend of hers named Mary who had helped sponsor Mother Teresa's first trip to the United States. Mary was very ill, so she wanted this visit.

Sr. Kathleen asked if I would like to drive her and the other sisters to St. Michael's hospital where Mary was staying. I was honored to be a part of such a blessing. I invited Myrna to come along and bring Liza. We got in our van and picked up Sr. Kathleen and the other sisters and proceeded to the hospital. I remember getting off the elevator and walking to the room where Mother Teresa was at the bedside of her friend, Mary. Mary looked almost asleep, maybe even making a bit of progress on her Heaven-bound journey. Then the most unusual thing happened, as we quietly stepped to the corner of the room Mother Teresa stood at the foot of Mary's hospital bed and held both of Mary's feet in her hands, shaking them and saying very loudly something I will never forget, "Mary, Mary, when you see Jesus, tell Him that I love Him."

The joy in her words, in her love for her friend, in her confidence of the existence of both Heaven and Jesus the Christ, and her childlike enthusiasm were such a gift for all of us to witness. Mother Theresa was celebrating with joy both Mary's life and Mary's passing by giving her a little assignment in Heaven.

I'm sure Mary delivered Mother Teresa's message and Jesus was more than pleased with their faith, as well as the knowledge that thirty years later I could share this inspiring lesson of faith, courage, and wisdom with you and your families. Imagine if we all had the childlike and yet strong faith of Mother Teresa and could follow her example by embracing a loved one's passing not as just a time of loss in this world, but also as a time of rejoicing for when "'He will wipe every tear from their eyes. There will be no more death' or mourning or crying or pain, for the old order of things has passed away." (Rev. 21:4)

CHAPTER TEN

Do You Want to Know the Sex of Your Baby?

During the scene showing Apple's late-term sonogram, two signifiant things happen: we see the preborn baby of Wanda, one of the shelter's real-life mothers, moving in her fifteen-year-old womb as she was the stand-in for Apple's pregnant belly. Also, the sonogram specialist asks "Do you want to know the sex?" and Apple smiles as she finds out she is having a girl.

Several Sources Shelters opened our first Crisis Pregnancy Sonogram Center in the Spring of 2013. Our Gift of Hope provides free ultrasounds, counseling, housing, motherhood training, baby supplies, emergency grants, and, most of all, we have counselors whose hearts are filled with God's love, mercy understanding, compassion and joy for this most important mission He has blessed us with over all these many years.

The Our Gift of Hope team consists of two sonogram specialists, a consulting doctor to help read the scans, a manager, two full-time counselors (one who speaks Spanish) and many wonderful and sensitive volunteers. We are open five days a week and have a website that lists free sonogram centers by state and offers free pregnancy tests for women who need them throughout the U.S. at www.ourgiftofhope.org

Several Sources opened its first crisis pregnancy sonogram center in Spring 2013. The name Our Gift of Hope was in inspired by an exchange of letters I had with Mother Teresa in 1988. My letter (Dated October 7, 1988) read:

Dear Mother Teresa,

I hope that my act in writing to you is not considered too bold. Yet act I must. For through prayer and meditation I feel the Holy Spirit guides my thoughts. And so I act not of my own will so boldly, but rather as I am gently moved by God's Loving Spirit.

There are many good people who are afraid to take that first small step for God. They await a sign from above. Yet they do not realize that God is within them. They search for God, in the sky with their eyes, yet do not realize that God is a Spirit and only their spirit can see Him.

Many good people are willing to travel for distances for God. Yet do not realize that He would rather have them simply bend down

> where they already live and help one in need. I feel that we sometimes live among kindly people who hesitate to act for God lest they appear foolish and face scorn and ridicule. They must remember that Jesus was also scorned and ridiculed for our sakes. We must now in these times face hostility and scorn for Jesus, and as He has taught us, we must bear it in silence.

I went on to explain how people had worked with me to open another shelter for pregnant women who needed a place to live so they could give life to their babies. I also told her that this shelter would provide support services after their babies were born. I explained that in front of the shelter we had a statue of the "Madonna della Strada," which shows Mary holding the Christ Child. The Plaque was to read,

"It is our hope that all who love Our Lady, and pray to her, keep gently in their hearts, Our Little Sister, Mother Teresa, and the Missionaries of Charity. Your prayers are asked for those who see in the eye of the poor the Face of Christ.
December 8, 1988.
This is the feast day of Mary's Immaculate Conception.

Mother Teresa responded to me in a handwritten letter from Rome dated 12/28/88 saying,

Dear Kathy DiFiore,

Thank you for your kind letter. I don't think you should use my name in the plaque. Why not name it "Gift of Love" or "Gift of Peace" or "Gift of Life?" I will pray for you all that God's blessings may be with you all, and remember—works of love are works of Peace. Let us pray.

God bless you.
Mother Teresa. MC

Mother's inspiring and encouraging letter came back to my mind twenty-four years later as I thought again about Mother's suggestions and was inspired to call our sonogram center, "Our Gift of Hope," for truly this is what the Center offers to women who decide they would like to see their preborn babies.

I can't help but wonder what Mother Teresa's reaction would be to seeing a baby's sonogram for the very first time. If you have not ever had the joy of seeing a baby in his or her mother's womb, I would encourage you to take the opportunity if you can. It is the experience of a lifetime. You truly will understand what the psalmist wrote when he said, "For you created my inmost being; you knit me together in my mother's womb. I praise you because I am fearfully and wonderfully made; your works are wonderful, I know that full well." (Psalm 139:13-14)

How I wish I could have you meet every one of the Several Sources mothers face-to-face and hear their individual stories. What I have shared here only scratches the surface. Over all these many years Several Sources Shelters has existed, so many people have come to visit us, and, as beautiful and precious as each baby is, it's the stories of their mothers that become the gift one can never forget. The confusion, the doubts, the stresses from a seemingly impossible unplanned pregnancy have turned into opportunities to start a new life together—a life with God's Most Holy Spirit to guide, protect, and comfort both mother and her child. And now that we have added this one missing link, Our Gift of Hope Sonogram Center, our mission, and the stories of the young mothers has become even more complete.

Lizette

Lizette found out she was pregnant and went immediately into panic mode. She just could not imagine having another child. Her son, Danny, was just a perfect little three-year-old boy. She had a good job, a car, and was living with her mother who could take care of Danny while Lizette was at work. This baby would upset her world in so many ways. While she didn't like the idea of ending her pregnancy, she thought this was her only choice. So, she made her appointment but she prayed, saying:

"God, can You please save this baby?" He answered my prayers when a woman in front of the

clinic handed me a flyer with a dove on the front. She told me about Gift of Hope Sonogram Center and I thought maybe God had sent this lady to me. So, I decided to walk across the street and learn about the program.

The people there were almost too nice. It was like it wasn't real. They were telling me about everything Several Sources did for the mothers, trying to make me feel secure and gain my trust. I was nervous, but relieved at the same time. They gave me many more things to bring home in a bag, but the most important things they gave me were my baby's sonogram photos. Words cannot express what seeing this baby gave me. There was a joy and happiness that touched my heart with a warm feeling I did not expect.

My sonogram photos gave me a deep connection to my child, knowing I couldn't let anyone harm her. I couldn't believe it! I felt this baby is a gift from God because her grandmother told me that God came to her in a dream and said that I would have a girl. At first, I thought she was crazy because my faith in God was never very strong. But when I saw the sonogram photos, and learned that I was having a girl, I knew that God had a plan. I started believing more in God. I treasure the sonogram pictures and have them hanging on the wall in my room. Now, every time I am in my room, I see the photos of my little girl and it gives me a reason to smile. I share the pictures with her father so he can know how I am feeling. At the moment of seeing my sonogram my decision to go to that clinic completely changed. I had now "met" my baby, and seen her, which is something I could never erase from my mind.

Sonograms are important because "meeting her baby" makes a woman feel closer to her baby. Women not seeing their babies, they don't realize or feel anything about how real this baby truly is. I would recommend that every pregnant mom who is thinking about ending her pregnancy get a sonogram first, because at the moment of meeting her little one, her mothering instincts will kick in.

I kept thinking about my son Danny, my sonogram, and all the promises they made. I thought God was answering my prayers after all.

For the time being, the people at Gift of Hope changed my mind. I was still confused about my decision, but about a week later I told my mom. She said she was not going to help me this time. I'm not staying with her if I have another baby. I decided to call the phone number on the card I received to see if there was still room for me and Danny. I took a leap of faith. The next thing I knew I was at the shelter.

I was thinking about adoption in the beginning to be honest. I was always against ending this pregnancy, but every problem pushes you in directions you don't want go like when I decided to make that appointment to end this pregnancy. Young women like me don't realize that there are other options, that you guys exist. So, that's what drives them to do something they will live to regret.

One of my most emotional days was when I spoke to the family who was giving me the grant to get my education. To this day have not met them.

The wife just kept telling me, "Don't worry. We got you." I was kinda emotional. She explained that they help a lot of girls here, but I kept thinking, "Who am I?" You don't even know me and you're going to help me with my education?

Lizzette just made the Dean's List with all As and one B. She just had classes in Terminology, Computers, a lab on Anatomy, CPR lessons, and medical procedures. She will graduate as a Medical Assistant with an Introduction to Nursing which is a nine-month program. She will be able to assist in phlebotomy and as a Certified Nursing Assistant. She could work for a hospital or clinic when she graduates in April 2014. Anyone who hires her will be blessed with an outstanding and very responsible employee.

Lizzette is one of many young women who have visited our sonogram center. I have personally been honored to counsel some of the women who come to Our Gift of Hope.

I remember counseling one young woman who needed assistance with paying a fee to obtain her Certified Nurses License. We got her a grant so she would be helped to move forward with her pregnancy and she would have the means to support her child. Every woman entering Our Gift of Hope receives not only her baby's sonogram photos and counseling, they learn about all our other support services. We give each woman a copy of the New Testament and a special little bracelet that says, "Pray Hard!" on it. God has helped and continues to help us do the work He has given us; and our commitment is to spread His word both in our actions and through the Holy Bible.

I must mention that the 4-D sonogram machine was donated to us by the Knights of Columbus, and we are very grateful for this wonderful gift which has helped us to save many babies' lives. We have dedicated our statue of St. Joseph in our "Garden of Life" behind our main shelter in Ramsey to the Knights of Columbus.

I have always loved the story of the birth of the Christ Child. Truly this story in the Holy Bible is the main focus of our work: helping mothers and their babies. Mary and Joseph had traveled to Galilee to be counted in the census and she was so close to delivery. They were far from home and their support system.

> While they were there, the time came for the baby to be born, and she gave birth to her firstborn, a son. She wrapped him in cloths and placed him in a manger, because there was no guest room available for them. (Luke 2:6-7)

So many wonderful similarities to inspire us beginning with that fact that poor St. Joseph and his dear wife, the Virgin Mary, had no place to give birth to the baby Jesus. How is it that the Son of God would be born homeless? Over this thirty-plus years I have wondered often how many lessons God was trying to teach us by having His Divine Son born with little more than His parents' love and concern. Was God, the Father, trying to explain through the birth of His only son that we too must be humble and obedient to His Will?

Mary and Joseph had to leave their home. They certainly would have liked to be home with friends and family around, but this was not possible. And so it is with our mothers. They do not want to come and live at a shelter with strangers, but in their case, this is the only option for delivering their babies. Mary waited nine long months and I can only imagine that she, like our mothers—like all mothers—not only physically connected with her baby, but did so spiritually as well.

I also wonder if she and Joseph had been able to have a sonogram, what that day would have been like as they saw the living preborn Son of God for the first time. Imagine if we had Jesus' sonogram images today to share. He who the prophets longed to see; He who freely chose to give up His rightful place in Heaven to come to earth to willingly sacrifice His Life on the Cross of Calvary, dying for our sins and reopening the Gates of Heaven.

God has blessed me with the honor and joy of supporting and comforting more mothers than I can possibly remember as they give birth to their precious little ones, and I can attest to the fact that no two are alike. But, the one factor that is common in all of them is that when they open their eyes and look at you for the first time you're probably as close to God's Holy innocent perfection as you ever will be in your life.

I'm sure Joseph and Mary felt humbled and in awe the very first time they saw the Baby Jesus. My guess is they could not take their eyes off of Him as they shared prayers of thanksgiving for a healthy baby boy. Both of them had been visited by an Angel so they knew Jesus was the Son of God. "An angel of the Lord appeared to him in a dream and said, 'Joseph son of David, do not be afraid to take Mary home as your wife, because what is conceived in her is from the Holy Spirit. She will give birth to a son, and you are to give him the name Jesus, because he will save his people from their sins.'" (Matthew 1:20-21). For them it must have felt like the world had stopped and the only place in existence was that stable as all the prophecies were now fulfilled and the next chapter was beginning.

New life has a way of doing that to every parent, which is why all of us here at the Several Sources Shelters are so very honored to serve those God brings to our doors. The work is our reward, and I would like to share with you a few more testimonials from women who have visited Our Gift of Hope Sonogram Center:

Maritza

I was about to go into the clinic, but something told me to turn around. I told the counselor as I was going in there, "I can't keep this baby." She was the only person who made me stop and think." She said, "We are here to help you. Just trust us." I felt something in my heart say, "Give her a chance to talk," and I said, "Okay, I'll give you thirty minutes." After seeing my son's sonogram, I cried and cried. I can't do this. They made me realize that there is a lot of hope out there.

I then got into a car with my nine-month-old daughter and two strangers and was taken to the shelter in Ramsey. I wondered if I was doing the right thing. I had just met these people. As soon as I saw the place, my heart was at peace. Everything was beyond perfect. I couldn't be happier.

The turning point was when I saw my baby's sonogram. I thought, Wow, God has planted this seed in my belly and God has a plan for us. *The sonogram helped me bond with my child more because I saw the picture and I knew it was real. It made me want to take it more easy, and slow. The kicks and movements now felt so special to me. Yes, I treasure the pictures because I keep them in my room, hanging up, knowing I have my baby boy. I was amazed!*

At first, I did not share the photos with anyone because I was scared of what people would say. I was scared and frightened to show my parents, because I did not know how they would react to my having two kids so close together, so young. Now my parents are happy and excited for the new arrival.

Sonograms are so important because women bond with their babies and choose life. It helped me change my mind, and it would help other women as well. Sonograms change women by giving them a reality check. They know they have a miracle inside their belly that they would have and cherish for the rest of their lives.

I realized that there was a lot of hope out there. I was sure my father would never let me back home with my second baby. Now everything is beyond perfect. I couldn't be happier. I decided to trust Several Sources and it was the best thing I ever could have done.

Since then, Maritza has been working full-time; her daughter has been in daycare; her baby is due in a few months. Once her son is a few months old she plans on taking advantage of our scholarship program to study online. She has two years of a college education and wants to complete her degree in business. Once her son is born and she gets through her first few months of mothering him she will apply for her scholarship from our Several Sources benefactors, and, taking one step at a time, through God's grace and guiding hand, her life will move forward. I wish you could meet her. She's just so full of fun and happiness. It's contagious and she is very smart. She's become one of our counselors at Gift of Hope and she's an inspiration to us all.

Candace

None of my family or my boyfriend were supporting my pregnancy and I do not have many friends, so I was alone when I went to the clinic. Then Betty suggested I have a sonogram across the street.

The first time I was able to see the image of my child, I froze and a tear came to my eye. Seeing the heartbeat really let me know there was a living person inside of me that I needed to take care of. Then, the ultrasound technician switched the image to a 3-D picture and I could actually see my baby's face in detail. I was told that I was having a boy. I cannot wait to meet him!

When I saw my son's face for the first time, I felt that I was in love! I will never forget that special day. The Gift of Hope team was so kind and supportive. I look forward to bringing my baby back to meet them so they can see what a wonderful job they do.

They even gave me all types of support services and now I know I can provide for my baby. My life is changing for the better because of Gift of Hope.

While sonograms or ultrasound machines didn't exist 2,000 years ago we do have the amazing experience of two preborn babies responding to each other. We read of Mary's visit to her cousin Elizabeth in Luke 1:39-40 when she shares with her the news of her pregnancy.

> At that time Mary got ready and hurried to a town in the hill country of Judea, where she Zechariah's house and greeted Elizabeth. When Elizabeth heard Mary's greeting, the baby leaped in her womb and Elizabeth was filled with the Holy Spirit.

The presence of the preborn Christ in the womb of His Virgin Mother Mary makes His preborn cousin John rejoice and leap in Elizabeth's womb. What a cornerstone moment in the history of mothers and their babies. These two men would soon be changing the world as their mothers watched and supported them. Many came to listen to them. Tiny preborn babies with a mission; sent here by God to change history. John would become the voice in the wilderness as he explained to the Pharisees, in the words of the prophet Isaiah: "I am the voice of one calling in the wilderness, 'Make straight the way for the Lord.'"(John 1:23). As a grown man, John would be a cornerstone of Jesus's ministry.

> "As soon as Jesus was baptized, he went up out of the water. At that moment heaven was opened, and he saw the Spirit of God descending like a dove and alighting on him. And a voice from heaven said, 'This is my Son, whom I love; with him I am well pleased.'" (Matthew 3:16-17)

Can you imagine hearing those same words "in whom I am well pleased" from God the Father? Should this be a goal of your day? Your week? Your year ? Your life?

The connection between Jesus and John the Baptist as preborn babies demonstrates the life that is forming in the womb and how that life has purpose and meaning that is predetermined by God. Sonograms allow us a look inside the womb to connect with that life and maybe catch a glimpse of the future God has planned.

> *Dear Lord, help us to be open to the will of the Most Blessed Trinity (Father, Jesus the Christ, and the Most Holy Spirit) as we seek to do your divine will today, tomorrow, and always. Help us to draw close to you each and every day of our*

lives. We ask this in Your Holy Name as we ask all Your Holy Angels, Your Saints, and Your Most Blessed Virgin Mary to join us. AMEN.

CHAPTER ELEVEN

Apple, We Have a Serious Problem

Life can be filled with problems and I always like to say, "A burden shared is lighter." So, when Kathy has to explain some of the difficulties surrounding Apple's minor status and staying without parental consent, things get very difficult between these two women who have a common goal but two unique personalities.

Many of our mothers have complicated problems, especially if they are minors and under the New Jersey Division of Youth and Family Services jurisdiction. This usually means that the state has intervened with their families for some reason. There is a delicate balance that sometimes requires the "Wisdom of Solomon."

This is why we established our Several Sources Special Families program nearly twenty-five years ago. Initially we the thought we would make this program available to our Several Sources mothers for emergency services until their child was eighteen years old. We never felt we could turn our backs on any of the mothers we took in, even after they left the shelter. I remember exactly the incident that prompted this decision. One of our mothers asked me this questions: "Kathy, why is there so much month left at the end of the milk? I just want to be able to give my children milk and every month when the last week comes, I just can't seem to make it happen." Those words kept haunting me. I always feel that God brings problems to me because He knows I'll try my best to do something with His help and inspiration to solve them.

Let me tell you a little bit more about how Several Sources originally started. I had attended Sunday Mass and the gospel that Sunday was about the miracle of the loaves and the fishes from Matthew 14:15-21 where Jesus feeds 5,000 people.

> As evening approached, the disciples came to Him and said, "This is a remote place, and it's already getting late. Send the crowds away, so they can go to the villages and buy themselves some food. Jesus replied, "They do not need to go away. You give them something to eat." "We have here only five loaves of bread and two fish," they answered. "Bring them here to Me," He said. And he directed the people to sit down on the grass. Taking the five loaves and the two fish and looking up to heaven, He gave thanks and broke the loaves. Then He gave them to the disciples, and the disciples gave them to the people. They all ate and were satisfied, and the disciples picked up twelve

> basketfuls of broken pieces that were left over. The number of those who ate was about five thousand men, besides women and children.

What an inspirational Bible story and since that day I am inspired to try to say yes to every idea the Holy Spirit brings my way, bit-by-bit. So, when the mother shared with me how difficult her life was when she ran out of milk for her children, our Special Families program began.

Now, seventy-four families with 168 children receive quarterly packages including food gift cards, clothing, school supplies, an inspirational gift, and a letter. Most especially, we want our families to know that their support is from Our Lord and their thanks needs to come from the children to God. These same families will call if they have a unique crisis or need. From time to time, a family has called to let us know that they no longer need our support and suggest others may be in more need.

As the years have passed, our special families program has grown, and I think I understand better the challenge Jesus gave us when He said, "They do not need to go away. You give them something to eat." I can almost hear Him say those words to me each and every day.

With His words and His actions, Jesus showed us what faith in God means. Heaven can be a part of our earthly life if we choose to live by Heaven's standards, by God's Divine gifts of faith, hope, and charity. Sometimes we just have to take that step forward knowing He is walking along side us, guiding us, inspiring us, teaching us, loving us as we try to do our humble part to follow His Word and His teachings found in the Holy Bible.

Jesus did not feed every single person in the world that day. He fed only those who were in front of Him. Maybe that is what He would like to see us try to do—help those we can in His Name. “Thy will be done on earth as it is in Heaven.” Over the years we have been blessed to help a few very special children (of course all children are special in God’s Divine eyes!).

Phoebe was born five years ago with a large hole in the lower part of her heart. Her father had died in Afghanistan before her parents were married. This left her young mother, Ashley, alone with no support system. Ashley found us on the internet and reached out for our help. Sadly the left side of Phoebe’s heart is not properly developed which causes problems in over 30% of her little heart.

I remember one time when poor little Phoebe needed another operation and Ashley was so frightened when Phoebe was in the operating room that she would not survive. She called me and asked me to pray because she had prayed in every corner of that hospital and had nowhere else to turn. Together we prayed on the phone and again Phoebe survived a difficult procedure.

We would help with local housing expenses for Ashley and, from time to time, rent or a light bill. How could we say no when a precious child was suffering and her father died in service to our county? So, we became their family and there was no turning back.

Phoebe has been on various medications her whole life and has had open-heart surgery more than once. She has to be constantly monitored and under a doctor's close supervision. She almost died when she was put on a heart and lung bypass machine. Phoebe has had so many complications in her short life that she remains undeveloped both physically and mentally. At five years old, she only weights twenty-four pounds.

Each month Several Sources pays $400 to purchase her nutritional supplements. Last year her young mother Ashley passed away of the same congenital heart problems and now Phoebe is being raised by her young aunt, Stephanie.

With very little financial means, Stephanie has asked for Several Sources to help fund Phoebe's needs that are not covered by insurance. Phoebe has a pacemaker but, recently had a surgery to replace the device due to ongoing problems that made it malfunction.

It is amazing that Phoebe is still with us today. Only a mother can understand what it's like to watch her child suffer. Ashley passed away, but from Heaven I'm sure she watches over Phoebe and her needs every day. There is no doubt in my mind that Ashley is asking Our Dear Lord to help her precious little daughter and to help us too as we continue to be a part of Phoebe's family here on earth.

Muneerah

Muneerah is also the mother of one of our Special Families. Her daughter, Jakiyah, is four years old and has been troubled with health issues since she was born. She has been diagnosed with asthma, acid reflux, and RSV (Respiratory Syncytial Virus), which is a virus that causes recurring respiratory infections.

Between these three conditions Jakiyah has been in and out of the hospital numerous times. Each time Jakiyah is about to be released from the hospital we receive a call from her mother asking for assistance to be able to purchase new bedding, cleaning supplies and special foods for Jakiyah's diet. A sterile environment is the key to a person being able to control a respiratory illness and is one of the stipulations for her release from the hospital.

These financial burdens put a strain on Muneerah's limited income. She knows that she can count on us for the additional support she needs. In September of this year doctors removed Jakiyah's tonsils and adenoids in hopes that this would alleviate some of her health problems. She has a breathing machine that she uses day and night to keep her respiratory condition under control. The constant use of this machine keeps the electricity bills extremely high. Some months it is a challenge for her to be able to pay the rent and the high cost of the electricity bill. Over the past year we have helped with both. We can't turn Jakiyah and her mother away as long as Our Lord gives us the means to continue to help her live.

Betty

When the maintenance man from "Ladies Rest" came in a few years ago to ask a special favor, little did we know that we would have the opportunity to help change and improve a young child's life.

"Mr. R," as he likes to be called, and his family had taken in an abandoned child, Betty, who, at eleven years old, badly needed eye surgery. He had no insurance. Mr. R wondered if he would be able to help Betty? Our Several Sources benefactors came through with the necessary financial aid. Now, Betty will not be teased at school and her good grades will be even better. God's love in action led us to a doctor who donated his services and benefactors who paid for Betty's hospital stay.

Michael

Michael was five years old when we met him. He was living in the Queen of Peace daytime shelter of the Missionaries of Charity with his mother Noreen. Sister Kathleen asked me if there might be anything we could do to help him and his mother, "He's so smart. I'm worried what will happen to him if they both continue to be homeless. "

As with all of our Special Families, we have continued to help mother and son for many years including housing them at one of our own shelters for a brief time. We help those who come to us to find an apartment, assist with a security deposit, food, furniture, and many other support services, not the least of them being our love, guidance, and concern.

In 1998, Michael attended our "Cruise to Celebrate Life" and one of our benefactors was very impressed with Michael's serious nature and love of school. After this, Michael's mother called us to ask for a special favor. "Can Several Sources help provide tuition to a private Catholic High School, Seton Hall Prep?" I was dumbfounded. Dare I ask the benefactor who showed so much interest? The benefactor from the Cruise said yes and, through God's Grace, we had our first Several Sources Scholarship student. Michael graduated in June 2003. He continued to receive financial aid through our Several Sources benefactor to attend Manhattan College and graduated in 2007. Michael went from complete homelessness to a college degree in a private Manhattan College, never having to pay a student loan. Today, Michael has a job in the field of advertising.

When I approached Michael to see if he would like me tell his story in this book, he had a surprising reaction. He told me he had read a very recent article about homeless children, detailing their sad and difficult lives in New York City and it made him think of me and all the he and his mother had because of being a Several Sources Family. He said, "You and the benefactors always looked after us."

As Michael was approving the copy in this chapter for you to read, he asked if he could come volunteer some of this time to help other children in need. What better way to end his story that to report that, as a grown man, he plans on giving back to other homeless children in need.

Amazing, simply amazing. God surely does work in strange and mysterious ways. One of the most thought-provoking parables that Jesus told was the one of the Good Samaritan who happened upon a man by the side of the road who had been beaten and robbed. The man had been passed over by two others who refused to help him. The Samaritan was considered to be an outcast, but he is the one who took care of this wounded man and paid for his recovery. Jesus was making a point about our responsibility to be good neighbors.

> "Which of these three do you think was a neighbor to the man who fell into the hands of robbers?" The expert in the law replied, "The one who had mercy on him." Jesus told him, "Go and do likewise." (Luke 10:36-37)

When I speak to our Several Sources mothers about this parable in Bible study, they understand its importance. They realize they and their babies are like the man who was attacked by robbers and our Several Sources Shelter is the Good Samaritan who takes care of them. Sadly, I too often hear, "I came here because there was nowhere else to go, but I didn't trust you." Over the years I have grown used to this thinking. They say, "Why would anyone do this for a stranger? Maybe you just want to take our babies from us." Some of our mothers have never been outside a city before and they'll say, "When we saw the forest (referring to the trees in our suburban New Jersey towns on the way to the shelter) I worried if I was being kidnapped." How sad that our culture has taken compassion, charity, and kindness and somehow transformed those noble qualities into fear.

Jesus said to his disciples, "The harvest is plentiful but the workers are few. Ask the Lord of the harvest, therefore, to send out workers into his harvest field."(Matthew 9:37-38). Jesus challenges us not just to identify with the "Good Samaritan," but to become the good neighbor. And let's switch roles for a moment and ask ourselves: if we were Phoebe or Jakiyah or Michael or Betty, who would we like to meet along our young and vulnerable life's journey?

Recently a magazine was interviewing me about *Gimme Shelter.* The writer wanted to know how people could get involved. I prayed before I answered her question and then suggested they start small such as going to their local church to see if they have a food pantry, then periodically conducting a food or diaper drive to help restock their pantry. Maybe they live in an apartment complex and know of an unwed mother who needs a stroller or a car seat? Just this week one of the unwed mothers I met on the internet was desperate for a simple car seat to bring her baby home in. She was a struggling student at UCLA and she couldn't find anyone to help her. I told her we'd get her the help she needed—such a small thing would be a heaven-sent blessing to this mother in need. If you want to get more involved you can contact any local charity and begin volunteering, or you can visit our website (www.lifecall.org) that lists shelters for unwed mothers and Crisis Pregnancy Centers. If you want to "dream big," go to our website and order one of our free "How to Open a Shelter" kits. You will find DVDs and the tools you need to start. We need more shelters for pregnant women everywhere. If they don't need volunteers they always need donations of baby supplies and, of course, funds. By the way, as I write this book we are desperately trying to reopen one of our shelters. If you are moved to help us in this area, you can contact us through the website to find out the best way to support this effort.

Be assured, if you pray and ask God for something to do for the least of these, you shall soon find that your prayer has been answered. Mine was and continues to be!

CHAPTER TWELVE

I Was Homeless Once

Gimme Shelter portrays a time when Kathy and her Several Sources mothers and babies attend a local church to request the financial support necessary to help her keep the shelter doors open. This pastor and the parishioners have become like family members to the Several Sources Shelters. Kathy spoke about the work at the shelter, but this time was different. She had decided to start by sharing some of her previously unknown, personal story. Apple listens carefully as Kathy explains how she, too, was at one time homeless.

Sharing this part of my real life was not pleasant and truly not something I wanted to do. Even now I hesitate to write about my personal story. I love to write or talk about my work because my work is a truly gift from God and my gift that I joyfully give back to Him in gratitude for allowing me to serve Him. When I think about my life I feel almost as if I have led two lives. One is the my life since Several Sources came into my world, and the other is a life from long ago and just “a book on a shelf” to be referred to once in a while as needed.

Because I do not want the focus to be on me, I must keep this personal part of my book short. I will simply share that I was married once. I suffered both mental and physical abuse to such a degree that the trauma of those years remains with me today. After seven years, I decided I had to leave. This decision meant being homeless for quite some time. Similar to most of the young women who come to our Several Sources Shelters, I had to move from friend to friend, embarrassed and ashamed.

I had one advantage: a good education. This allowed me to secure a job which enabled me to eventually buy a small home. God surely does “write straight with crooked lines!” We simply must have faith and allow God to be in control. We must quiet our hearts, our minds, and our souls and pray for His Holy Spirit to help us decide which step we should take next. It amazes me how often a young mother or a homeless woman from “Ladies Rest” will open up her heart and begin to trust our Several Sources Shelters once she finds out that I was once homeless and even abused like so many of them have been. Their eyes seem to say, “If Kathy can do it, so can I!”

This sense of sisterhood—this hope and mutual understanding—somehow begins to plant a seed that they too might help other women to realize God is always with them every hour of the day.

As you know I started Several Sources when I gave our dear Lord “a blank check” to do in my life what He would. And, with the Holy Bible, the Lord's Prayer, and the life of St. Francis of Assisi as my guides, I stepped out in faith. One of my favorite miracles is found in John when Jesus begins His ministry. He attends a wedding in the town of Cana with His disciples and His mother is also in attendance.

> When the wine ran out, the mother of Jesus said to Him, "They have no wine." And Jesus said to her, "Woman, what does this have to do with me? My hour has not yet come." His mother said to the servants, "Do whatever he tells you." . . . Jesus said to the servants, "Fill the jars with water." And they filled them up to the brim. And He said to them, "Now draw some out and take it to the master of the feast.". . . The master of the feast called the bridegroom and said to him, "Everyone serves the good wine first, and when people have drunk freely, then the poor wine. But you have kept the good wine until now." This, the first of his signs, Jesus did at Cana in Galilee, and manifested His glory. And His disciples believed in Him.
>
> —John 2:1-11

Over the years the lesson that I learn very time I read or mediate on this miracle is not about Jesus turning the water into wine, but that His mother instructed the servants, "Do whatever He tells you."

I think about those words with every decision I make as I gratefully try to do the work He has given me through the Several Sources Shelters. The fact is, while the apostles had the joy of being in His divine presence, today we must depend on our faith, and most important, our knowledge of His Word to know how He thinks and what matters to Him. Again and again, the life of St. Francis, the life and the letters of Mother Teresa, and the words of Jesus help me to focus and re-focus my life's priorities. He offers His "Blueprint to Heaven" for us in Matthew 25:35-40:

> For I was hungry and you gave Me something to eat, I was thirsty and you gave Me something to drink, I was a stranger and you invited me in, I needed clothes and you clothed Me, I was sick and you looked after Me, I was in prison and you came to visit Me.
>
> Then the righteous will answer him, "Lord, when did we see you hungry and feed you, or thirsty and give you something to drink? When did we see you a stranger and invite you in, or needing clothes and clothe you? When did we see you sick or in prison and go to visit you?" The King will reply, "Truly I tell you, whatever you did for one of the least of these brothers and sisters of mine, you did for Me."

So, I pray and I look for His Most Holy Spirit to inspire and direct me as I set our Several Sources priorities and channel our resources into the place that He would like them to be.

This is why when Sr. Kathleen called and asked for help with any homeless pregnant women who might need a safe place to stay, I said yes. And as our relationship grew and I began to realize how difficult her mission was in serving the homeless women and children of Newark, I finally asked, "What can I do to help?"

She asked for a place for the homeless to go during the day—hopefully to find jobs and eventually find permanent housing.

I had to take some time to think and pray. I already had a 24-hour-a-day ministry for our unwed mothers and their babies. How could we do this? Then I remembered a lesson God taught me early in the history of Several Sources, "Kathy, if the request be from God— like the water being turned into wine—the same will happen for you."

So, we took baby steps, and in June of 1989 Sr. Kathleen and I approached Fr. Harvey Balance who was the pastor of Queen of Peace where both the sisters and the homeless ladies lived. We asked if Several Sources Shelters might be allowed to use a small part of the church basement as a daytime shelter for the women who slept at the Missionaries of Charity nighttime shelter called "Queen of Peace." We started out part-time and, day-by-day, we could see and experience the lives of the homeless women and children improving. We would have food, baby supplies, a warm, clean, safe place for the women and children to come during the day; but, most of all our love, our compassion, and our friendship.

Why was this so important? Twenty-four years ago Newark was going through very difficult times. Poverty and crime were part of every day life. Also at that time, the sisters were allowed to house both women and children. However, they would have to leave the shelter at 6:30 am only to see cars of the drug dealers and pimps waiting to lure them into dangerous and unwanted activities. My desire to help meet Sr. Kathleen's request for a daytime shelter became more urgent as I learned more of what she and these women were up against. Thinking about some of the stories of poverty, suffering, and loss still breaks my heart to this very day. Thanks be to God, the pastor, Fr. Balance agreed, and our little rescue mission for God's poor, homeless, and needy women and children of Newark began.

For many years, Several Sources volunteers had been working in the church basement and using vans to help the poor and needy of the inner city. In 1997, the years of serving were blessed with the opening of our fifth Shelter called Ladies Rest in Newark, New Jersey. Three businessmen with kind and generous hearts pledged to pay the rent for the first three years. We had to raise the operating expenses. Now, Several Sources Shelters has a daytime shelter for homeless women of all ages.

Ladies Rest is a daytime shelter for homeless women. It is needed to complement nighttime shelters in Newark, where the homeless are only allowed to sleep. Our Ladies Rest program offers a homeless woman the dignity and helping hands she needs to put her life back together. Imagine for one moment what it is like to be homeless. The nighttime shelter staff tells you that you must be out by 7AM and cannot return, no matter the weather, until 4PM. The public library isn't open. If you want to go to the bathroom, all you can do is hope the local coffee shop will let you use its facilities. There is a long day ahead. They won't let you loiter in the bus station or the train station. You're scared and very alone.

Then someone tells you about "Ladies Rest." It sounds like Heaven! They offer food, warmth, clothes, training, telephones, a fax machine, an opportunity to learn about computers, a mailing address—and more important than all this, love, hope, counseling, and a God-centered haven to call "home." Yes . . . HOME—a new start, a fresh beginning, a reason to try harder to put your broken life back together. No fees are ever charged. Bible study, discussion groups, and prayer are daily-shared experiences.

At the Ladies Rest we encountered those who have gone through many of life's struggles—hopelessness, depression, loss (parents or child), addiction to alcohol or drugs, abuse, diseases like cancer and AIDS. These women have gone through tragedies most of us can hardly imagine.

Those who come to Ladies Rest experience so much pain on a daily basis. They arrive at times with hospital bracelets still on their wrists. It is a devastating sight. But many are experiencing a pain that medicine can never relieve. They look at you with unseeing eyes. They are lost and hopeless. I can not know how it feels to be sick and homeless, wanting to lay your head and curl up in your bed and close those tired eyes yet not having that option. It sounds so simple, but is like heaven to imagine for them. We apportioned a room on the third floor for just this purpose, providing beds with clean sheets and pillows for those who are so tired and physically unable. We wake them up to eat, but they would rather rest. They are able to sleep because they feel safe.

The ladies who come regard Ladies Rest as home—a safe place, good food, good company—but, above all, they come to learn that there is a God who loves us and who knows what we are going through. And to those who will persevere, He waits for us and prepares a mansion unlike no other.

We are very happy when we can share a very good meal during the holidays. With the meal we usually have the joy of sharing God's Love. We share our blessings and pain. We thank God because we are still here. And we pray for those who made it possible for us to be here. We pray with St. Francis of Assisi: "Lord make us an instrument of Your Peace." AMEN.

When twins Mary and Martha first came to New York City to find a better future together, they fell on hard times. They found themselves without work and homeless. Eventually, they found a place to stay with the Missionaries of Charity nighttime shelter in Newark, NJ, and the nuns there referred them to our daytime shelter at Ladies Rest as a place they could find the additional help they needed.

Ladies Rest saved our lives. It gave us hope, love, safety, and joy that we hadn't had in many years. Miss Charlotte is one of the most excellent people we have ever met. We were made to feel comfortable and safe. She took care of us like her own. She basically took our pain away.

— Mary and Martha

In the last several years, Ladies Rest has also become a "Babies Rest." The mean and dangerous streets of the inner city have given mothers and grandmothers the idea to come to Ladies Rest with their children to simply play in a safe environment and have a free hot meal. Clothing, school supplies, prayer, and Bible study are found in abundance. Gone for a few hours are the fears and dangers of daily life.

Words cannot express how invaluable this Blessed House has been. It has been a transforming factor in my life, from the daily bread of the food (which is always blessed before we eat it) to the weekly "bread" of the Word of God visited upon us by the visiting Sisters from St. Lucy's Church in Newark. People in the "street community" continually comment, "You look better;" "Where you been hangin'?;" etc. (I want to tell them, "Under the shadow of the Almighty," because that's what it feels like).

A thousand thanks would not come close for this safe haven, for this oasis in chaos, for a dry place from "the storm." Honestly, without this place, I do not know what I would be now, but because it is here, I can feel even closer to God than I've ever felt in my life. I feel changed . . . and changing, going toward what God wants to mold me into. Thank God for your vision. With love.

—Laura

Ladies Rest is a God-centered haven for lost and hurting souls. It is an answer to the hopelessness and despair experienced by women without a place to live in the inner city.

Ladies Rest means to me "Shelter From the Storm" figuratively and literally. For three years, I slept out in the street. How does it feel to save somebody's life? How does it feel to save – wow – somebody's soul? A person you've never met. A stranger. Not anymore."

—Laverne

Ladies Rest offers a homeless woman dignity and a way out of the broken cycle of poverty and despair. It is a place where a homeless woman can rediscover that she matters; that God loves her and that people do care.

My name is Monica. I've been coming to Ladies Rest for several years. Ladies Rest has provided me with shelter during the day, when I might have wandered aimlessly throughout Newark streets hungry and tired. Ladies Rest helps me renew my strength and faith in God and my fellow man.

I've gone from homeless to a nice apartment and part-time job. Ms. Charlotte has been God-sent. She is loving, nurturing and compassionate. She helped me regroup my life and have faith and confidence in myself again. I would've been lost without Ladies Rest and Ms. Charlotte.

I can never thank you and Ladies Rest enough. There have been times I have mentioned Ladies Rest functions to people who are not involved and have no need for such an organization. These people are astounded by all the help, love and services made available for homeless women. God bless Ladies Rest and Thank You.

—Monica

Several of the homeless women we have helped through our Ladies Rest shelter have mentioned Miss Charlotte. Our shelter manager, Charlotte Florentino, is a self-giving woman whose attitude toward her role in Ladies Rest is as follows:

"I am more blessed when I serve them. [to the women] I get more out of serving you than me giving you something, because everything that I share with you is not mine. It's from the Holy Spirit. Every time we have food on the table we pray. We ask God to bless those who made it possible for us to come here every day. I am only an instrument. Praise God."

The homeless women come not only for a safe place to stay, but also for help in putting their lives back together. The women are given clothing, provided with financial aid for medicine, transportation to job interviews and, if they are unable to work, they are helped with social services and encouraged in every way possible to become independent and self-sufficient. Prayer, spiritual support, and guidance are an important part of each day.

Maria is another woman who came to us at Ladies Rest. She was screaming and crying uncontrollably as she came into the door of the shelter for the very first time. Charlotte didn't know what to do. Marie seemed out of control. She thought of calling the police, but somehow she could not. She also thought about calling the psychiatric screener hotline for people who are thinking about causing bodying harm to themselves or others. Someone would come to Ladies Rest with a professional who would screen Marie right there. Marie mentioned that she wanted to kill herself and her husband, too.

Charlotte decided to bring Marie into her office and then noticed for the first time that Marie was wearing hospital bracelets. Charlotte did not know now how wise it would be to take Marie into Ladies Rest, but she continued to pray and finally got Marie to calm down a bit. Marie finally shared with her, “I just found out my husband has given me AIDS. I have a twelve-year-old daughter. What am I going to do?” Marie had married her husband three years ago. She had been sick the past couple of months and decided she needed to see what was wrong. Now her world was falling apart. Charlotte, although shocked, kept asking the Holy Spirit for His help and gave Maria a hug as she said, "I can not help you with this disease, but I can tell you that God loves you as He loves me."

The fear and anger that were consuming Marie seemed to subside a bit as Charlotte continued, "All of us will die someday." Marie looked at her and said simply, "I know." Charlotte continued, "I am also going to die. I don't know what I am going to die of, but if you kill him or yourself what will happen to your daughter? You have to think of her too. How will you take care of her? Let's say a special prayer together now." And so they prayed the prayer Charlotte always prays when there is trouble at Ladies Rest and she must counsel one of the our ladies:

> *"Come Holy Spirit, fill the hearts of Thy faithful and kindle in them the fire of Your love. Send forth Thy spirit that they shalt be created and thou shalt renew the face of the earth. AMEN."*

That was the turning point of this poor woman's anger which was based on fear and despair. Since that day, Marie has visited Ladies Rest four times. She is now divorced. Physically and mentally she has gotten better and better. She has a purpose in life now—to speak about her disease and tell people that there is hope. Because she is bilingual, Marie can minister to many of those in need of her help. She says, "It is more about Jesus loving us. Jesus loves you in spite of the fact that you have AIDS. AIDS is of the body, not of the soul. I am so grateful I found Ladies Rest that day. I came filled with anger, and, as I left, I felt at peace."

Charlotte explains, "I will never forget her because it made me happy that she is more at peace now. She could have gone home and had a very bad argument and done some thing terrible. Things could have been different for her and her young daughter who could have need up with out parents."

Marie's comment about being at peace is what we strive for at Ladies Rest. During the Last Supper Jesus says, "Peace I leave with you; my peace I give you. I do not give to you as the world gives. Do not let your hearts be troubled and do not be afraid." (John 24:27) Later that night Jesus explains to the Apostles about how His relationship with them would soon change and how God in the Most Blessed Trinity would continue to be available to them,

> "But I tell you the truth, it is better for you that I go. For if I do not go, the Advocate will not come to you. But if I go, I will send Him to you. And when He comes He will convict the world in regard to sin and righteousness, because they do not believe in Me; righteousness, because I am going to the Father and you will no longer see Me; condemnation, because the ruler of

> this world has been condemned. I have much more to tell you, but you cannot bear it now. But when He comes, the Spirit of Truth, He will guide you to all truth. He will not speak on His own, but He will speak what He hears and will declare to you the things that are coming. He will glorify Me, because He will take from what is mine and declare it to you. Everything that the Father has is mine; for this reason I told you that He will take from what is Mine and declare it to you." (John 16: 7-15).

The strange thing is that when I came to pick up Ronald Krauss the very first time he visited our Several Sources Shelters, I brought him a book about miracles and on the gold cover of the book was a beautiful white dove, the symbol of God's Most Holy Spirit. To this day I don't know if Ronald has read the book, but I have come to believe with all my hear that *Gimme Shelter* has both an earthly director (Ronald Krauss) and a Divine director (The Holy Trinity). How else could all the blessed things have happened come together to make this film become a reality? My mind flows with ideas and thoughts which I will place in the final chapter, but please know that the Holy Spirit is always available to you every hour of the day, in every struggle in your life, every challenge, every opportunity, every decision. Ask yourself this: Why would I move forward on any decision without God's advice if all I had to do is text Him or give Him a quick call? That's now available to you simply through the power of prayer. This is how my life and so many other lives have unfolded. Please join us as we continue to live in Christ's Peace.

Now, I would like to introduce you to a few more of our Ladies Rest family members. I hope you enjoy meeting them because they are a part of your family now. Every time the mothers, the women from Ladies Rest, the volunteers, and the staff meet, we pray for you and your family. Just by your support of this book, you have become a part of our Several Sources Family. Please pray for us as we pray for you, as stated in the "Our Father," Thy Kingdom come. Thy Will be done. On earth as it is in Heaven. Amen. (Matthew 6:10).

My name is Mavis. I used to be on drugs and I was tired of that life, so I came to "Ladies Rest" and Miss Charlotte gave me a Bible. I want to say thank you so much for having a place and staff like you have. You and your staff have saved my life, and you gave me my life back.

I go to a drug program every day and I take my mental health medicine. Without your program I didn't have money to use the phone and find a program that could help me. I have gained ten pounds. I read my Bible every night and I am free of drugs. Thank you very much for giving me my life back.

– Mavis.

Ladies Rest provides use of a computer, phone, office supplies, a washer and dryer, and the professional and business support our homeless ladies need to get on their feet, but most of all it offers compassion and hope.

My name is Charlina. I've been coming to Ladies Rest for the past couple of years. I know without your love and dedication, there would be no Ladies Rest. I am very grateful to have had the opportunity to come here. I am also very grateful for everything you have done to help us in our time of need.

I didn't have much before being able to come to Ladies Rest. I was in a shelter. It really wasn't easy every morning having to leave at 7:00 and not having anywhere to go or any place to get a hot meal. I deeply thank you for everything. I really don't know what I could do to repay you, but I do feel that I could help others as you helped me.

I don't know where I would be without Ladies Rest. Also to have the love form Miss Charlotte and the love and help from you, Miss Kathy helps a lot. I have a wonderful feeling in my heart to know that there's a place where the less fortunate can be helped. I just really wanna say I love you. I love Ladies Rest and also thank you for helping me in my time of need.

– Charlina.

In 2013, we served 107 ladies and one child. We focus on ladies who are from Mother Teresa's shelter on Jay Street in Newark. They have a maximum stay of twenty-one days—never enough to put their lives back together, especially when they are devoid of identification because of situations such as their bags being stolen while they were at Penn Station or thrown away from their most recent residences when they were evicted. We assisted six ladies in reconstructing their identities by applying for their Birth Certificates, Marriage Certificates, or Social Security Cards, and by providing the Ladies Rest address as proof of residence.

Two of our ladies are legally blind. They do not have Medicaid or any medical insurance. They applied for Charity Care. We assisted with medications that were very expensive because insurance will not pay for them. We provided one with a cane, eye drops, special eyeglasses, and a magnifying glass. We applied for Social Security Disability for one and the other is still being assisted in acquiring identification papers.

My name is Desira. Thank you for paying for my eye drops. I have glaucoma and high blood pressure in my eyes. I do not have medicare and charity care will not pay for my medication. Thanks to you I have started to do what I need to do now to get my welfare case opened.

Three of our ladies have been approved for and signed up with Section-8 housing. They get their own room and don't have to worry about utilities. One of our women, Suzanne, is in her second year at Essex County College. She was living at the YWCA in Newark, subsisting on her student loans. She came to Ladies Rest one day to see if we could give her lunch. When Charlotte learned about her situation, she realized Suzanne fit the "homeless" description. Now, she comes to Ladies Rest so she can have decent food. We replaced her dilapidated backpack, sneakers, and provided bus fare. She'd been struggling to make both ends meet. She was very grateful, saying, "I hope to make it one day."

Without Kathy keeping this place open, what would we do? She is a blessing and I will never forget what Ladies Rest did for me. I thank God for sending Kathy and Charlotte into my life, 'cause I would be doing drugs and alcohol and wouldn't be taking care of myself without Ladies Rest. Kathy is blessed and God gave her to women that are in need and don't know which way to turn or go. I'm ending this letter with love, peace, harmony, care, and blessings with all my heart and thank you very much. May God bless everyone at Several Sources.

—Zelma

Pam came to Ladies Rest in 2001 two weeks after her twenty-three-year-old daughter passed away from an unexpected stroke. Pam was a nurse at Englewood Hospital in Teaneck, NJ. Her daughter's death made her loose the desire to live, and one day she decided to pack up everything in her apartment in Cliffside Park and come to Newark without having a place to live.

She arrived at the Missionaries of Charity Queen of Peace night time shelter in Newark deeply depressed. Mother Teresa's Sisters suggested that she visit Ladies Rest as is the procedure at Queen of Peace. Sister Kathleen partnered with Several Sources Shelters so the homeless women of Newark could have some dignity and access to much needed services such as the use of a phone, assistance in reconstructing their IDs. Ladies Rest opened in 1997, There have been seven mother superiors since Sister Kathleen's request and countless daily occasions where Ladies Rest has brought to life the words of Jesus, in Matthew 25, "When I was homeless, you took me in. What you have done for the least of these thy brethren, you have done unto Me."

When Pam came to Ladies Rest for the first time, she indicated that she had no where to live beyond the twenty-one days that the homeless women are allowed to stay at the Queen of Peace nighttime shelter. At the very same time Queen of Peace needed a live in Housemother and the sister's asked Charlotte, our Ladies Rest Manager, if there was anyone she could suggest. Charlotte suggested Pam who was deeply spiritual and had a strong personal relationship with God. She was immediately accepted and stayed for four years. Pam said, "The homeless women would return from a day at Ladies Rest full of hope, happiness, and talking about their joy-filled experiences there."

The distance from the nighttime shelter to Ladies Rest was only a two or three-block walk. The ladies were excited about the training opportunities, the chance to earn their G.E.D., and most of all, the permanent housing opportunities which we would search out and provide for them.

They love the Bible study at Ladies Rest because many of them have not known real love in their lives. They begin to realize that God came in the presence of His Son Jesus the Christ to love them, teach them, and ultimately die for them so the gates of Heaven would be re-opened for them and for their families for all eternity.

His deep love took away their feelings of doubt, of fear, of not being unwanted. They began to understand that God truly considers them His daughters who He loves, and he is constantly seeking to hear their voices lifted up in prayer to Him every hour of the day.

We focus on the fact that Jesus loves them and some of the woman of Ladies Rest have become more involved in local churches, (most especially St. Patrick's Pro-Cathedral which is the parish where Ladies Rest is located. Several Sources functions out of this church's old convent. Several of the women have completed Catholic Rites of Christian Initiation of Adults (RCIA). We focus on Christ's love and so for the ladies who are of other faiths, we encourage them to bring back their personal relationship with Jesus the Christ by resuming their involvement with the church of their faith. In essence, Ladies Rest becomes a place for spiritual insight, knowledge of God's Holy Word, and hopefully a healing of past injustices and abuse. They come to Ladies Rest and find God's love in action.

Unfortunately Pam had to have spiral surgery three times. She called Charlotte to see if we could help her find permanent housing. As she left Ladies Rest, Pam said to Charlotte, "Ladies Rest is a safe haven of Peace and Christ's love for the homeless women of Newark including me. As the Housemother of Queen of Peace nighttime shelter, I simply do not know what I would have done without Ladies Rest for all the homeless women we helped over the years. And now you are helping me too, not only to apply for disability, but to find permanent housing! How can I ever thank you? Know that I will be praying for you and your works of mercy for God's children in need, especially the homeless, battered, forgotten, and suffering women of Newark."

Pam is one of our great success stories. It is so rewarding to be able to help women through difficult times in their lives and restore their hope.

Please join us in prayer that the work and the mission of helping the needy homeless and poor women of Ladies Rest will continue for many years to come.

A few Christmases ago, I was attending one of their many celebrations and decided to take a photo of the manger scene that Charlotte always places out at the Ladies Rest entrance during the Christmas holiday. The strangest thing happened. There is a white image of a Dove moving across the scene of baby Jesus, His Virgin Mother Mary, and her devoted spouse, Saint Joseph. I have included this photo in the photo insert so you can judge for yourself. Pray and hopefully God will send His Most Holy Spirit to you with His Divine answer. As for me, the answer is in the words which Jesus spoke to the apostles after His Resurrection before His ascension to Heaven, as He commissioned them saying, "Therefore go and make disciplines of all nations, baptizing them in the name of the Father, and of the Son and of the Holy Spirit, teaching them to obey everything I have commanded you. And surely I am with you always, to the very end of the age." (Matt. 28:20)

CHAPTER THIRTEEN

I Have a Special Announcement

One of my favorite scenes in *Gimme Shelter* is when Kathy and all the mothers and their babies go to a local diner. The owner, Dino is treating them to a fabulous dinner. Everyone is having a great time when Kathy announces a special upcoming celebration.

In 1988 a mutual friend asked me if I would help a group called The United Nations Women's Guild to design their 40th Anniversary Exhibit at the UN. They were having some issues and needed guidance and special support in order to assist children in need and support mother-child care programs throughout the world. The Guild had started in 1948 shortly after World War II as a small all-volunteer woman's organization. The Exhibit was a great success and, in appreciation, I was made a lifetime member and given support for the possibility of Several Sources Shelters becoming a Non-Governmental Organization (NGO) of the United Nations.

I thought and prayed about the opportunity and could not help but wonder how such a small organization could be given such a large opportunity. I wondered if this truly was within God's plans for us? As I often do when faced with a new situation, I turned to Holy Scriptures. This time I found an example of how Jesus expanded his ministry in the gospel of Luke. "After this the Lord appointed seventy-two others and sent them two-by-two ahead of him to every town and place where he was about to go. He told them, 'The harvest is plentiful, but the workers are few.'" (Luke 10:1-2) So, if Jesus could send His disciples two-by-two, maybe Several Sources could follow His leadership example and do likewise.

Both United Nations Women's Guild and Several Sources were established to help children and their mothers, so we had a common bond and mission. With God's help, together we would do even more for His children in need. By becoming an NGO, Several Sources might be able to expand our mission.

One of my favorite passages, Matthew 7:18-20, would definitely confirm this decision, "A good tree cannot bear bad fruit, and a bad tree cannot bear good fruit. Every tree that does not bear good fruit is cut down and thrown into the fire. Thus, by their fruit you will recognize them." With time our relationships with both organizations would help us determine if this was part of God's Divine plan for the Several Sources Shelters.

In June 1999, Several Sources Shelters became an NGO of the United Nations with both

National and Special Status. NGOs participate in the work of the UN, are able to be part of the legislative process through conference participation and new issues raised by NGOs in public sessions at the UN. We were involved in many activities, but two of them were so critical that they bear sharing with you.

Chernobyl Children

On April 26, 1986, an explosion and fire happened at the Chernobyl Nuclear Power Plant. It released large quantities of radioactive particles into the atmosphere, which spread over large portions of the western USSR and Europe. The Republic of Belarus suffered the most damage.

The Chernobyl disaster is considered to be one of the worst nuclear power plant accidents in history. Over 500,000 workers participated in containing the contamination to avert a greater catastrophe. Long-term effects, such as cancers and deformities, are still emerging. There was extensive radioactive contamination in the area, and people from a nineteen-mile zone around the power plant were evacuated from their homes.

Through the sponsorship of the United Nations Women's Guild (UNWG) eight children who were victims of the Chernobyl accident visited the US for three weeks in March of 1998. These children, who range from 9 to 12 years old, were suffering from leukemia as a result of radioactive contamination. The four girls and four boys from the Republic of Belarus traveled with a pediatrician and an interpreter. The pediatrician, Sergey, reported that all of the children had cancer and malignant tumors.

One of their first activities was to stay overnight at the Several Sources Shelter in Ramsey. A Several Sources benefactor underwrote the expenses for one of the children and another Several Sources benefactor sponsored a trip to Washington, DC for all of the children. After visiting Several Sources, they went shopping for sneakers and visited a mall in Paramus. The physician explained that getting new sneakers was a very special opportunity for them.

Ghana Quarry Children

In June, 2001 Several Sources participated in a United Nations Preparatory Committee for the Special Session of the General Assembly on children. During the session, we heard about situations throughout the world that involve needy children. We would like to be involved in each of them, but with limited resources, we decided to focus on helping the quarry children of Ghana.

These children work for four cents a day using only their bare hands and hammers to break stone in the quarries of Ghana. The money is just enough to buy one meal. They have no protective gear because their hands and eyes are too small. Some have nowhere to sleep but the concrete streets of Ghana.

The children, ages 4 to 17, are taken from their parents with the promise of an eventual education. Instead, all the children find is a 12 to 15-hour day of labor in the quarries. Pregnant women also work in the quarries. The dust is cancerous, yet the workers breathe it in daily. These child laborers break stone with only a hand held hammer. Sometimes they cut off their own fingers and pieces of stone go into their eyes causing the loss of vision in that eye.

In one orphanage there were 384 of these quarry children. Several Sources Shelters decided to figure out a way to make protective gloves for the children and get goggles for their eyes. Aside from this protection for their bodies, Several Sources was encouraged to help with their schooling. The orphanage manager was building a library room, but there were no books for the quarry orphans. For my birthday I went to Barnes and Noble to find books that featured black children. We were blessed to find someone who would ship them for free.

Several Sources purchased protective gloves and goggles for these children thanks to the generosity of our benefactors. Now, you may be saying to yourself, "Why did Kathy involve herself in another project when there is so much to do here?" All I can say is that I felt the Holy Spirit asking me to get involved and in my heart. I just couldn't bear the thought of knowing that there were children we could be helping and then do nothing to help stop their suffering.

Ukraine-Uganda Gift of Hope

In 2011, a Ugandan college student in the Ukraine learned about Several Sources through the Internet when she was pregnant and did not know what to do next. Prim was in school studying to be a doctor and away from her homeland of Uganda. We were able to help her get a sonogram where she learned she would have a daughter. After a number of e-mails and with time and prayer, Prim decided to give birth to her baby girl and, thankful for our help, she chose to name her after me, calling her Katrina. She e-mailed me when she saw her baby's sonogram.

> Dear Kathy,
>
> Finally I have the photos. Katrina is very healthy. She is so active. In those pictures you will see her head fully developed—the eyes, nose, mouth and ears are so clear. Actually her whole body is clearly seen and all is very ok with her. Thanks to Several Sources I bought myself a new winter jacket as my Christmas present. Thank you so much Kathy. We love you and always wish you the best.
>
> Prim and Katrina

Our correspondence continued and a very positive and supportive relationship emerged. On March 17, 2012, Prim gave birth to Katrina and wrote this thank you letter to Several Sources and our benefactors.

> When I was pregnant I did not know where I would get help from, but kept on trusting in the Lord. I looked for help in many different organizations but failed to get any. Not until

one day when I came across Several Sources Shelters. I e-mailed to them telling them about my situation and how I needed help. I was so surprised by the quick response from Kathy. This is when I got lost hope back. Kathy always kept on telling me please pray and whatever you do plan on giving the gift of life to your baby, and I did exactly what she told me. She told me that all things are possible if we lean on God. And that is exactly what I did.

For sure I had no help at all, since I had no job. Kathy supported me in so many ways, especially spiritually. I thank God for leading me to Kathy for she is for sure an angel sent from heaven to save. I continued as a volunteer saving babies in my community by counseling other pregnant women as Kathy has taught me and Several Sources gave me the grants I needed to proceed through a healthy pregnancy while helping other pregnant women I would meet. This was a partnership made in heaven.

Now when I look at my beautiful baby daughter, Katrina, I feel so special and loved by God. She is an angel to me. I'm glad I named her after Kathy. This will keep memories of how she was saved alive for years to come. I love it when she makes me busy all the time—bathing her, feeding her, dressing her, and playing with her. I feel happier than before. I'm so thankful to God

> and Kathy and the Several Sources benefactors They are the reasons why I'm fulfilled, happy and at peace now.

Prim not only decided to choose life for her baby, she was asked to consider opening a Gift of Hope Crisis Pregnancy Center in the Ukraine to help support women who might also be pregnant and desperately in need of help. After some support and training from Kathy, Prim has been saving baby after baby after baby in her homeland, Uganda, through contacts and friends, and in the Ukraine where Prim continued her education. This is a simple grass roots mission to help young women choose life for their preborn babies with local pregnancy counseling and the ability to offer baby clothes, diapers, bedding, and food. Prim is an inspiration. I received this lovely email from her.

> Dear Kathy,
>
> You cannot believe this; the Holy Spirit is with us. I have a friend on face book. I could always read her status updates and they were always negative thoughts about life. I kept wondering why she looks at life that way. I prayed to God for her to see light. One day I decided to have a chat with her. We talked about several things and I told her about the GIFT OF HOPE. I asked her to read about our page on face book. Today, I was chatting with her and she opened up to me

about her two and half month pregnancy. She was confused and upset, because her boyfriend no longer cares for her and he needs no babies now.

I told her about my story and several other stories about the babies Several Sources saved. I'm so glad she is now keeping her baby and consulting with me about how to keep her pregnancy healthy since I am in medical school. My heart is full of happiness because of you and Several Sources. Many babies are saved because of you. May our good Lord give you good health.
GOD BLESS

– PRIM

Sarah

Sarah was four months pregnant when she learned of Gift Of Hope in the Ukraine. She approached me through a friend and Prim helped save her baby, this made her feel better since Sarah had heard testimonies from her friend before.

Sarah's major problem was isolation. She did not know how the society would accept her with a child and not being married to the father. Prim helped her realize that her opinion about her future mattered more than what the rest of the world would say about her.

Prim kept on translating the articles Several Sources sent about the saved babies for her into Russian. Sarah read all the stories and simply changed her mind. She kept her baby and now her parents are helping her out with the baby as she continues to study. Amazing how other women's decisions halfway around the world were able to save Sarah's baby's life.

Ellen

Ellen heard about us through a testimony Prim gave in church about how she had found out about Several Sources and how we helped Prim save her pregnancy. By then Ellen was confused on whether to keep the baby or not. She approached Prim after Mass and asked for help because she saw how determined Prim was to keep her pregnancy. Prim gave her scriptures to reference to make her strong and to help her face the challenge together with God. Her friends were definitely against the pregnancy because it was a shame to them to have her still in their clique and pregnant.

Prim talked to her friends and asked them to support Ellen in this most trying time. At first they saw Prim as a joke, but Prim trusted the Lord and believed that all would turn out well for Ellen. After two weeks, the friends decided to help Ellen out—took her for pre-natal care and even helped her with the lessons in class she had missed.

In fact, they organized a baby shower for her and bought her very precious presents. Whenever she had class, one of her friends took care of the baby. Now Ellen is back in Nigeria, her home country, with a Masters in Pharmacology. Her parents found out about their grandson at the airport when they picked her up. She wrote to say how happy they were. Amazing how such little things can save a baby! That is why calling our pregnancy centers “Gift of Hope” is truly a perfect name.

Angela

Angela got to know of the Gift of Hope Center when Prim was braiding her hair. She had been wondering who to consult as far as her pregnancy was concerned, because her boyfriend did not want to support this child due to their economic status. When she opened up, Prim advised her to keep her baby because that is what really matters most. Prim and Angela took a walk in the park, and as they spoke, they saw mothers carrying their babies. Tears ran down Angela’s face. Prim asked her to think about missing motherhood and the joy of watching her child grow.

Angela still hesitated. Her boyfriend had already made an appointment with the clinic for early the next morning. When Angela arrived at the hospital, she had second thoughts and right away told her boyfriend she was going to keep her baby. He broke up with her and she had to face the responsibilities alone.

Prim kept on telling her to cast all her burdens to God and not to lean on her own understanding. Prim kept on talking to her. She was inspired, because Prim was also pregnant while taking care of her. When Angela talked to her mother about her pregnancy, all hope returned. Angela and her baby now live with her mother in Nigeria.

Lynne

Prim's classmate introduced her to Lynne. Lynne's father died was she was fifteen years old, and now she was abandoned. She was nineteen but not really ready for this baby in her life. Prim tried counseling and telling her Christ will see her through but she kept on saying "But, I don't have a good job. Even the one I have already is like a burden to me." We kept in prayer and faith. She travelled back to her city but still with the thought about what to do. She called Prim after a month to say her uncle who lives in Germany will be taking care of Lynne and that she will be living in Germany with him. She got a job there and she says all is well now. Our prayers were answered.

Ritah

Ritah, mother to Isaac, is Nigerian but studies in the Ukraine. She and Prim had a mutual friend, who told her about the Gift of Hope center. Ritah was experiencing a lot of depression and stress. She wanted to end her pregnancy. When Prim got to know about her situation, Prim told Ritah her own story. At first, she just could not believe it, until Prim showed her Katrina's sonogram picture that Kathy had paid for.

She was so encouraged and together they began saving for the baby's needs. They organized a baby shower for her together with her friends who whole-heartedly presented her with gifts. The baby was born and now lives in Nigeria with his grandparents.

Patricia

Patricia lives in Sweden but is Ugandan. She heard about the Gift of Hope Life Center through our page on Facebook. She wrote how she was facing difficulties with her mother-in-law who did not want this baby to be born. Her mother-in law called her a "gold digger," because she was from a poor family and her son is rich.

She had been living in such conditions since she was two weeks pregnant, crying into her pillow every night. Prim asked her to refer to Joshua 1:9 "Have I not commanded you? Be strong and courageous. Do not be afraid; do not be discouraged, for the Lord your God will be with you wherever you go." They kept praying together and Prim asked Patricia to trust in God. Now Patricia's husband is so supportive, her mother in-law is out of her way because her son is determined to take care of his wife.

All of these examples of helping pregnant women and their babies both born and preborn halfway around the world are a living testimonial to Jesus' words, "For where two or three are gathered together in My Name, there am I in the midst of them." (Matthew 18:20). How else could one explain people coming together from all different backgrounds to support these needy women and children with little to no support except their prayers, good will, and faith? Psalm 40:8 says, "I desire to do Your will, My God; your law is within my heart." I think this is the common bond among all these women and those who, against all odds, struggle to have their babies, just as young, sixteen-year-old, Apple does in *Gimme Shelter*.

Please contact us if you would like to start up a Crisis Pregnancy Center in your area. Together with God's help we'll begin the process, or you can venture out on your own. Prim did so in two countries, almost at the very same time. You would be amazed how caring and concerned people can be, especially when a baby is involved. Diapers, strollers, car seats, baby clothes all just seem to arrive even without solicitation. Why would you want to get involved in this or any other activity for a needy person now or in the future? I believe the answer is found in Matthew 25:31-46. The essence of it follows, but I pray you will take the time to read and study the entire passage.

> Then the King will say to those on His right hand, 'Come, you blessed of My Father, inherit the kingdom prepared for you from the foundation of the world: or I was hungry and you gave Me food; I was thirsty and you gave Me drink; I was a stranger and you took Me in; I was naked and you clothed Me; I was sick and you visited Me; I was in prison and you came to Me.' . . . 'Assuredly, I say to you, inasmuch as you did it to one of the least of these My brethren, you did it to Me.'

Just as Jesus recognized those who did for "the least of these," he did not acknowledge those who passed over those in need. Something to think and pray about indeed. I truly believe these words to be true and try my best to live by them and to teach our Several Sources mothers to do so as well. And my hope is that they teach their children, too. I always tell them when we conduct our bible studies that we have two reasons for doing so. We want them to get to Heaven and we want them to teach their children by their example and through studying the Holy Word of God how to live their lives so that we all may have a big reunion in heaven with all present and accounted for.

Let me end this international chapter with a positive message from Mother Teresa's letter of Dec. 28, 1988 from Rome,

> Dear Kathy DiFiore,
>
> Thank you for your kind letter. I will pray for you all that God's blessing may be with you all. And remember – works of love are works of Peace. Let us pray.
>
> God bless you.
> M. Teresa, M.C.

CHAPTER FOURTEEN

See You Suddenly

In the film, Kathy uses the phrase "See you suddenly" as a way of saying goodbye. She first says this when Fr. McCarthy introduces her to Apple. They have a brief chat, and when Kathy explains to Apple that they will meet again tomorrow, she ends with "See you suddenly." This phrase is used again by Kathy when Apple appears to be permanently leaving the shelter to go live with her father.

"See you suddenly" is something I have heard over the years on the streets of Newark by both young people and not-so-young people. The words are hope-filled versus saying "Goodbye." The words have a sense of joy, uncertainty, and drama to them, which in many ways are symbolic of not only my mission at Several Sources, but my lifestyle, and, ultimately, my work for God.

"Suddenly" is a word frequently used in the New Testament, and I think "suddenly" is often how God works in our lives. If we, in faith, turn our lives over to Him and ask Him with all our hearts to walk with us every hour of the day, we will find Him there with us. Like parents who would guide their child and hold their hand to be sure no harm would come to that child, God will place "Suddenlys" in our lives.

One of my favorite "Suddenlys" is in Luke 2:13-15,

> Suddenly a great company of the heavenly host appeared with the angel, praising God and saying, "Glory to God in the Highest, and on earth, Peace to those on whom his favor rests." When the angels had left them and gone into heaven, the shepherds said to one another, "Let's go to Bethlehem and see this thing that has happened, which the Lord has told us about."

A multitude of angels delivered this message of hope and salvation to the shepherds and "suddenly" the world was changing. Two thousand years later, that "Suddenly" event is still echoing in the hearts and minds of men and women throughout the world, but we are not as fortunate as the shepherds. They got to see a "host of angels." They got to hear those angels praising God.

There is a Christmas scene in *Gimme Shelter* when Kathy has the shelter mothers and their babies stand on the steps in our actual shelter's great room. The sign on the steps holds the words the angels sang that first Christmas night, "Glory to God in the

Highest, and on earth, Peace to Men of Good Will. (Luke 2:14)" While we have taken this photo many times in the real world of our Several Sources Shelters, we have on a continuous basis had to explain to our mothers that God is always with us—every day, every hour.

This is one of the most difficult parts of the work at Several Sources. So often, our mothers come to us broken and confused by their former lives, and like Apple in the film, they doubt whether God really even knows or cares about them. "Suddenly" has to become "permanently" and "continuously" for them to understand God's ever-constant love and peace—the moment-to-moment grace—that can be theirs even in adversity.

God and His divine presence arrives in the most unusual places and at the most unexpected times. For me, receiving that fine back in 1984 on my birthday, my world was "suddenly" changed. To be honest with you, when I got the letter, I laughed out loud at God's sense of humor and said to myself, "Now it begins." I just knew that somehow God was behind this whole thing. I didn't know where His plan for me and the mothers and babies would lead, but I did know I would follow. I had given Him that blank check for my life. There was no way I was going to look back. I had to step forward in faith. Just like the little girl who is stuck in the tree, when her Father says, with his arms extended, "Jump, I'll catch you," I was about to jump.

I thank God for my Italian grandmother whose love for Jesus was the guidepost in my life.

Her instruction and what I learned while teaching religious education on Sundays to children have given me the biblical foundation I needed to get me through the many challenges I've encountered.

Recently, someone commented that they wanted to know more about what "makes me tick." They seemed perplexed by my answer. It was one word: God. I'm not married. I have no children. For thirty-three years, I have chosen step-by-step, day-by-day to be exclusively with Him through the work He gives me—sharing His love and fulfilling His mission to serve His children in need.

"Suddenly" seems to be part of God's style when we become involved in His Plans. Jesus' life and ministry was filled with miracles that happened suddenly.

> Then he got into the boat and his disciples followed him. Suddenly a furious storm came up on the lake, so that the waves swept over the boat. But Jesus was sleeping. The disciples went and woke him, saying, "Lord, save us! We're going to drown!" He replied, "You of little faith, why are you so afraid?" Then he got up and rebuked the winds and the waves, and it was completely calm. The men were amazed and asked, "What kind of man is this? Even the winds and the waves obey him!"
>
> —Matthew 8:23-27

What a powerful miracle. Imagine if we could have been in that boat. I can't help but hope that "suddenly" we would believe in the living Christ who has dominion over nature and has saved our eternal lives. Yet, so many of those men who witnessed this miracle would, in the coming days, deny they knew him. Once again they feared for themselves and their earthly needs and desires. And from the cross, Jesus would say those most merciful words, "Father, forgive them, for they do not know what they are doing." (Luke 23:34)

First we are to "become the message," and then we need to follow His divine example. He taught us to forgive. So, "suddenly" forgiveness is the key that opens the everlasting graces, which abound from God's mercy.

This is a lesson that is very difficult to apply in our daily lives and many of the young mothers who come to the Several Sources Shelters struggle with forgiving and feeling forgiven. Our mission and role at the Several Sources Shelters is to help our young mothers find God's divine plan for them. In doing so, we encourage them to make Him a daily part of their life's journey. "Trust in the Lord with all your heart . . . and He will direct make your paths straight." (Proverbs 3:5-6)

I share with them three little prayers that I pray every day.

Lord, help me set my priorities. Amen.

This one is very simple. This was my prayer the very first day that I found myself doing God's work full-time. I had made a list of things to do the night before. I remember there were nineteen items on the list. Shortly after I woke up, the phone rang. Someone was answering the ad I had placed in the local paper looking for a spare bedroom and they were interested in taking in an unwed mother. She wanted to know if I still needed help and if I had a booklet describing my program. The answer was, "Yes, I need the spare bedroom because my house is full; but, no, I don't have a booklet." That was the day I realized that I needed my "Lord, help me set my priorities" prayer. And He is both creative and faithful in answering my prayer.

My second short prayer is my "Two-by-Four" prayer:

Please, Lord pick up one of your two-by-fours and hit me over the head. I promise to immediately do whatever You ask of me. AMEN.

My third prayer is the shortest.

God, give me strength. AMEN.

I say this one often throughout the day as I move through my responsibilities, which seem endless at times. This last prayer truly is meant not for me, but for those we serve at Several Sources Shelters. Our devoted staff and benefactors, through God's ever-constant graces, make our work for our mothers, their babies, the homeless women of Ladies Rest, and our Special Families children possible.

Going back to "What makes Kathy tick" . . . for the first seventeen years of Several Sources, my work was the most fulfilling and important part of my life as I strived to do exactly what I thought God wanted me to do—help His children in need, particularly those who are Preborn. "Suddenly" I was faced with a new problem, a personal crisis that urgently needed my attention. I was diagnosed with cancer and would need immediate surgery as well as intensive chemotherapy.

These treatments extended my life by five years. Then I was told the cancer had metastasized and I would be facing more surgeries and additional chemotherapy. But through God's grace another miracle happened and I became eligible for a new cancer drug which I continue to receive. This ongoing treatment is necessary because I have a condition where 2 million cancer cells grow in my body every three weeks.

I go to the hospital regularly to receive a treatment that destroys the cells that have grown since the last visit. So, as I sit here typing I notice my next treatment is in ten days. There really is no side-effect to this medication except I must get my heart check ed a multigated acquisition (MUGA) scan every six months to be sure there are no problems developing. If that happens, I might have to stop the treatment and that would most likely mean I would have six months to live. But, my doctor has told me this is unlikely since I have had no heart problems in the fifteen years I've been receiving the treatment.

This battle helps me focus on doing things and making decisions in a way that would please God. If you knew that you were living three weeks at a time, what priorities would you set for yourself? Every single time I leave the hospital doors, I say to God, "We've got three more weeks. Do with me as you choose!" Fifteen years of that lifestyle can make you pretty deliberate in doing what you think God has called you to do, and it's really not hard to be focused on being a good person when you know your time might be very limited.

Twice the cancer has spread to my brain requiring surgery, and that is how I met Dr. Liza DeAngelus, head of Neurology at Memorial Sloan-Kettering in New York City. One of my favorite sentiments comes from Liza: "Kathy, we have to fix you up good, so we can kick you out the front door, so you can save more babies!" I love that philosophy.

In early March 2011 when Ronald had written the script, cast the film, and established the shooting schedule, he decided that he wanted to film *Gimme Shelter* at our Several Sources main shelter and that was quite an honor. But something was wrong. I was having trouble with my balance and my vision on my left side. I knew I needed to see Dr. D'Angelis. She quickly gave me an exam and that same day arranged for me to see a neurosurgeon. I was scheduled for brain surgery on April 4, 2011 and the filming was to start in June 2011. I asked the surgeon if the operation could be delayed until after the filming. His response was, "We need to get you in here as soon as possible."

Okay, I guess God was helping me set my priorities again.

My concern was that Ronald Krauss, the director, had a plan for me to handle recruiting background cast for the movie from our Several Sources past, present, and future babies. Our little ones would be appearing in the actual movie *Gimme Shelter*. Three of our mothers were selected to perform in the film, and I was supposed to help them with their schedules, childcare, and keep them company when they were on the *Gimme Shelter* set.

Reluctantly, I made the call to Ronald letting him know of my situation. He was concerned, shocked, and truly wondering if the filming should be delayed. I assured him that it was only going to be a three-day hospital stay and that I had plenty of time to recover. I just knew God would not have brought *Gimme Shelter* this far and then not allow me to do my small part when I was needed.

On my way to my MRI the day before surgery, I said a prayer of thanksgiving for the medical team that God had recruited, for all the prayers from our Several Sources mothers, staff, and benefactors, and for my successful surgery and speedy recovery. I don't remember anything about the actual surgery, but I do remember asking my friend and co-worker Sharon Ross to get me ice chips. She told me later that I was giving directions to a number of the nurses and hospital employees. I didn't make any sense with what I was telling them to do, but I was directing anyway. When I came a bit more to my senses, I asked Sharon to get Ronald on the phone for me. Ronald didn't recognize my voice at all, but eventually he figure out that it was me post-anesthesia. I just kept reassuring him that I was fine and that the filming should go on as scheduled.

The day after the surgery, I was assessed for cognitive abilities, peripheral vision, overall general motor skills, and started occupational therapy. As it turned out, thanks be to God, I recovered so fast that I was allowed to go home one day early. All of my prayers and the prayers of everyone who cared about me were answered. This certainly bought to mind the Bible verse, “Jesus looked at them and said, ‘With man this is impossible, but with God all things are possible.’” (Matthew 19:26)

The Several Sources housemothers who drove me home teased me as I left the hospital and happily prayed to God, “I’m leaving one day early. See you suddenly. AMEN. And a thank you to Dr. Gutin for saving my life!” I had decided that instead of staying home, I would recover at our convent shelter. For me, this was a good plan because I would be surrounded with the mothers and babies who had become not just my work, but also my family. I did not realize how upsetting it would be for the mothers to see me for the first time after my surgery. When I arrived so happy to be out of the hospital I needed help going up each step of a small flight of stairs. Later, I learned from one of the housemothers that this was hard to watch because they all knew me as a strong and independent person.

Life at our shelters can be very intense, but there are events like this one that burn in your memory. During the time that I was dealing with the legislation issues, I walked past the open front door of my home and saw three pregnant teenagers, (Anne, Anna, and Lillian) who didn't always get along, with their arms around each other. They didn't know I was watching them as they cried saying, "What's going to happen to us if this place closes?" Up to that moment I had focused on solving the problem, but God was now opening my eyes to the fact that my responsibilities also included ministering to these broken-hearted pregnant teens. I called them into the living room and reassured them that "everything was going to be just fine. Yes, we have a problem, but God is with us and He will help us. Now, more than ever, we need to be a family and support each other. We will grow in love and in strength as long as we realize that God is by our side."

As I came home to recover in 2011, I saw this happening. When God is at the center, crisis brings people together instead of dividing them. The bonds of family unity are so strong that one can feel the presence of God's healing spirit in the room.

As I was greeted at the front door by seven-month-old Xavier in the arms of his eighteen-year-old mother, Erin, God was filling my world with healing joy. Xavier smiled and clapped his hands and kept reaching to touch the big bandage on my head. As I got into the kitchen I realized every Several Sources mother, baby, and staff member was there to greet me. The "Welcome Home" signs and flowers were quite touching. The mothers took turns asking me how I felt and telling me how glad they were to see me. Their words and their concerns meant more to me than any banners, flowers, or decorations. The mothers updated me on the current events at the shelter while I was away.

The next day I explained to the mothers that I would have to go through occupational and physical therapy. I let them know that a therapist would be coming to the shelter. The mothers actually volunteered to help me through my exercises and two of them helped me with washing my hair once I was allowed to do so. I remember asking them to count my staples just before I returned to Dr. Gutin's office to have them removed.

One of the mothers named Princess asked if she could see me in private. She wanted to share with me a dream she had where I was in a wonderful field with wild flowers wearing a white gown with a very long train. I was holding a baby, but the unusual part of her dream was that the train of the gown went for miles and miles, and on the train she could see countless beautiful babies. She then asked me if her dream could be made into a Several Sources painting. I promised her I'd think and pray, asking God what He thinks of her idea. Princess then introduced me to a new mother named Amesha. She had arrived just the day before. She told me that she heard about Several Sources through the antiviolence hotline and she was still questioning her decision to come stay at our shelter.

I shared with her some of our Several Sources literature and she commented that she really can't feel anything yet. I tried to explain how at eleven weeks her baby is so tiny she might only feel a flutter from-to-time. Amesha then explained to me that her baby is due on Thanksgiving, her birthday. I told her how special this would be that they could celebrate their first Christmas together this year. Amesha was scared and I encouraged her to be strong. I told her we would be strong for each other. We have lots of love.

I asked Amesha if she'd like me to be her labor and delivery coach and asked Princess to share with Amesha her dream. Amesha's reaction was a bit of a surprise to Princess and to me. She simply said, "My baby would be the smallest."

The next few days were filled with therapy visits and more fun with the babies. The next important event was when Darlisha and Allyson accompanied me on my hospital visit to have my fifty staples removed. This was the first time that the young mothers had been at Memorial Sloan-Kettering and they seemed happy but a bit leery while they waited. Although they were allowed to accompany me, they were not permitted to see them remove staples or be with me when I heard the blessing that my biopsy was completely negative. Dr. Gutin had become more than my doctor, he was my friend and lifesaver.

God had used his hands, his mind, and his talents to save my life so I could go on to save more babies. He was my hero and hero of the countless others Several Sources would be able to help in the future. I thanked Dr. Gutin for saving my life and he thanked me for my Passover card and the few photos I gave him of our Several Sources family. I will forever be grateful that God put us together so that I might continue the work He called me to do.

In searching for a way to end this very personal and complex chapter of *Gimme Shelter*, I am inspired to share with you a portion of the letter Mother Teresa wrote to me from Calcutta on December 9, 1988. Her words echo in my heart and soul as a call to greater holiness not just for me, but for all of us.

> Dear Kathy,
>
> Keep up the good work you are doing. I pray that God may flood your soul with His spirit and life, so that you may radiate His love to all you meet. God love you and bless you for the love you give and the joy you share thorough your gift to God's poor. Keep the joy of loving through sharing. My prayer for you [is] that you may grow more and more in the likeness of Christ through love and compassion and so become an instrument of peace.
>
> God bless you.
> Mother Teresa, MC

Epilogue

Over the thirty-three years that Several Sources has been in existence some of the people benefitting from our labors have been pregnant women, mothers, and their children. Some are the homeless women of Newark, others have been young children with serious health issues. Our work has also reached needy children through the United Nations Women's Guild. Our faith-filled mission has always been in harmony with the words of Christ, "What you have done for the least of these thy brethren, you have done unto Me."

It took me six weeks to write about thirty-three years of work that hopefully will be pleasing to Our Lord. Whether it be a success in man's eyes, we have yet to find out; but, I do know that the many women and children who have benefitted from the work of Several Sources Shelters are pleased that we exist to this very day and hopefully for many years to come.

A couple of week ago, as I was trying to get through a very busy schedule, there was almost no time to sleep. My "To Do" list was much too long given the time frame to accomplish all that was on the ever-growing list. After two days of struggling with the list and trying to figure out with God's help what was most important, a strange thing happened.

I had finally gotten a good night's sleep, and as I lay in my bed, before I could even open my eyes, in my heart I heard the words, "Be Noah." I thought, "How strange. First, as a woman how could this relate to me? And, second, how could a biblical event that happened tens of thousands of years ago relate to me? Again, in my heart, I heard the simple sentence, "As God called the animals two-by-two to the Ark, so He shall help you." WOW. That was quite an amazing idea—a new way to look at my faith in God and learn to trust Him more. He has never given me more than I could handle before. Why would He begin now? I just had to relax, take a deep breath, pray, and practice on "being Noah" a bit more often. Two things struck me about this message: One is that the very first item I ever purchased in 1981 for my home to honor the work was a collector's plate of Noah's Ark with the animals featured on it; and, of all things, that very plate somehow was in the living room when we shot the scene where Monsignor McCarthy brought Apple to the shelter for the very first time to meet Kathy. I also thought that if I could benefit from the "be Noah" message or lesson, maybe some of the people reading this little book might also benefit. Don't be afraid to venture out and try to do something for God. He'll be right by your side. As you struggle with your godly priorities, He will help you set and meet them, if you ask it of Him.

One of my most treasured possessions is an item also shown in *Gimme Shelter* when Fr. McCarthy first brings Apple to the shelter. Mother Teresa's Missionaries of Charity were going to throw out a statue of Jesus at the age of twelve preaching to the Pharisees. The reason they were discarding it is the statue had no hands. Sr. Kathleen graciously gave the unique statue to me. This may seem odd, but I loved the message in it. Only three people have ever correctly guessed why. It is because *we* must become *His* hands. We must do His works of Love, of Mercy, of Compassion, of Forgiveness in this troubled world. We are hands when we offer shelter or when we reach out to a person who is ill. We are His Divine Hands reaching out to everyone. People often ask me, "Kathy how many babies have you saved? How many mothers over all the years have you taken in? How many homeless women and children have you served? How many needy children have you helped over all these many years? Basically, how many times have you served God?

My answer is always the same: "I am not an accountant or a bureaucrat working with numbers. The counting I leave to God and His Holy Angels." But one memory from the production of the *Gimme Shelter* film that I will never forget is from the night of the "wrap" when we were preparing to shoot our final scene. We were in Newark filming a nighttime scene when I received an urgent call. One of our sixteen-year-old mothers named Wanda was in labor and I was her birthing coach. We had used Wanda as a double for Apple during the scene when she had her second sonogram. Her preborn son, Jordany, actually can be seen turning in his mother's belly. Ronald also used a recording Jordany's first cries after his delivery in the scene when Apple's baby, Hope, is born. His presence in the film brought our total number of Several Sources Shelter babies featured in the movie to twenty-four. As for me, I know in my heart I'm supposed to focus on the work. As Mother Teresa said so well in in letter to me in January 1990, “Pray the work.” And, as I have tried to follow her example, I have had a special request of God that when I get to the place He Has prepared for me in Heaven (John 14:2) that the walls of my house would be covered with the photos of all those I have helped in His Holy Name so I could learn and understand better His Divine mercy. And I have one other request. Could He somehow have prepared for me a film that would have the moments in my life that He treasured most? I just can’t imagine what they would be, but I think such a gift would be a blessing for each and every one of us. I hope you agree.

Wouldn’t you like to ask Him for a similar display of your photos and your own video of what He valued most in your life? I’ll invite you to see my collection and hopefully you’ll do the same for me!

“Ask and it shall be given to you; seek and you will find; knock and the door shall be opened for you.” (Matthew 7:7)

I would be remiss if I did not tell you that "saved" baby Faith (Erika's daughter) was born on January 19, 2014, exactly on the day I finished this book. And you know what Erika decided to name her baby? Faith. That is the message behind each and every chapter of this book. We all must allow God's Divine Mustard Seed of Faith to grow in our hearts, minds, and souls so we can become His instruments of peace, love, and joy in this troubled and needy world. Welcome to the world little Faith!

As God used you to inspire us, may you continue to be an inspiration to all you meet in your lifetime. AMEN.

Acknowledgements

Each day I start with this prayer. "For myself Lord, I ask nothing, save that You send Your Most Holy Spirit unto me, so that I will have knowledge of Your Will. Amen."

To do His Divine Will, many blessing have been and currently are being given to me.

First I'd like to thank my parents, my family, and my Several Sources Family.

I thank all the bishops and Archbishops who have allowed us to speak at their churches all these many years.

I thank our Several Sources benefactors past, present, and future who have helped us to keep our shelter doors open as the work continues.

I'd like to thank Mother Teresa and President Reagan for their friendship and loyalty to the work of the several Sources Shelters.

I thank all the mothers and babies, homeless women, and needy children who we have served overall these many years.

And I'd like to thank Ronald Krauss for his dedication and tireless work in making the story of *Gimme Shelter* come alive through an excellent cast, crew, and team of experts. Ronald's commitment to making this film could never be topped. I pray that *Gimme Shelter* becomes more than a film. I pray the movie becomes a movement that inspires people to help each other take the focus off material things and put their energies on helping (as the Good Samaritan did) the people in need who

God brings before you. I pray the message is well received and thank God, many Angels, and Saints.

I'd like to end with a little story about my dear father. Dad passed away in his early 80's of Alzheimer's. I was his caregiver as my dear mother was suffering from both Parkinson's Disease and the early stages of Alzheimer's as well. One night I had to go to a dinner with a few benefactors and as I left the nursing home, I gave my Dad a kiss on his forehead and said to him, "I love you." I then told him, "Dad, you're supposed to say back, 'I love you too.'" He looked at me with that Alzheimer's stare of confusion, as if trying to figure out if I was his nurse, his friend, or his daughter. Then said to me, "I love you threes." My father had a severe stroke the very next day and a passed away soon after. So, the last words he said to me— words I will always treasure—were, "I love you threes."

It makes me think of one for the Father, one for the Son, and one for the Holy Spirit.

That is how I feel about all of those in this Acknowledgements section of my book as I say , I love you threes and thank you all and close with this prayer for you and your dear families:

Prayer of Consecration to the Trinity
O everlasting and Triune God, I consecrate myself wholly to you today. Let all my days offer you ceaseless praise, My hands move to the rhythm of your impulses, My feet be swift in your service, My voice sing

constantly of you, My lips proclaim your message, My eyes perceive you everywhere, And my ears be attuned to your inspirations. May my intellect be filled with your wisdom, My will be moved by your beauty, My heart be enraptured with your love, And my soul be flooded with your grace. Grant that every action of mine be done For your greater glory And the advancement of my salvation.
Amen.[9]

9. http://www.catholic.org/prayers/prayer.php?p=2164

Resources

http://www.severalsources.net - explains the mission and activities of the Several Sources Shelters

http://www.goldencradle.org - source for adoption services

http://www.singleandparenting.org - single parent help center

http://www.chastitycall.org - how to teach teens about chastity

http://ourgiftofhope.org - Crisis Pregnancy Center offering free sonograms in Northern New Jersey and a link to those offering the same in other states

www.lifecall.org - help for pregnant women in crisis, link to shelters nation wide

http://www.heartbeatinternational.org - help & support for pregnancy centers

http://birthright.org - services for those in crisis due to unplanned pregnancy

http://www.severalsourcesfd.org/several-sources-open-shelter.html - guide for opening a shelter for pregnant teens & young women http://rachelsvineyard.org/index.html - Rachel's Vineyard for those suffering traumatic loss

http://nurturingnetwork.org - help for pregnant college students and those working full-time

http://theunchoice.com/men.htm#resources - support for fathers in need of healing

http://www.youtube.com/watch?v=erb3p9Ifbxg&feature=em-share_video_user - development of the baby week by week

http://www.biblestudytools.com/topical-verses/- search the bible by topic for answers

http://www.helpguide.org - help with domestic abuse & violence, addictions, mental & emotional health issues

"Ask and it shall be given to you; seek and you will find; knock and the door shall be opened for you."

—Matthew 7:7

About the Author

Kathy DiFiore, Founder of the Several Sources Shelters received her Undergraduate Degree in Psychology from the University of Rochester in 1969. In 1979, she received her MBA from NYU and in 1989 received an Honorary Doctorate Degree from Felician College. She is currently studying for her doctorate in Education at the University of Phoenix online. As a devout Catholic, Kathy bases her life on the prayer of St. Francis of Assisi and Matthew 25:40, "What you have done for the least of these thy brothers, you have done unto Me."

From 1970 to 1978 she was a member of the NY State Advisory Committee to the U.S. Civil Rights Committee. Her business career included holding the position of Personnel Director, American Express, Credit Card Division and Personnel Director at Degussa Chemicals Corporation. In 1981 Kathy decided to turn her own home into a Shelter for mothers and their babies. As the demand for her help for pregnant women grew, Kathy made a decision to leave the corporate world and devote full time to helping mothers and babies in need. She is now operating four residential shelters in New Jersey, a 24-hour national hotline 1-800-662-2678 for pregnant women, and five informative websites. Several Sources also has a fifth shelter called "Ladies Rest" in Newark, NJ for women who are homeless and in need of daytime help to get back on their feet.

In 1998, Kathy was honored by being invested as a Dame of Malta and received at St. Bonaventure University, the Gaudete Award for her continuing work on behalf of our mothers and their babies. Other Awards include the NJ State Council of the Columbiettes "Humanitarian of the Year" Award in 1989, St. Elizabeth's College Catholic Woman of Achievement in 1995, and the Pax Christi N. J. Dorothy Day Award in 2001.

In March of 2005, Kathy received the Dr. Martin Luther King, Jr. Award from the United Methodist Church of Newark, N.J. for her work in the inner city of Newark for women and children in need. In 2007 Kathy won the Abstinence Clearing House Impact Award and had her first research article published in the California Journal of Health Promotion. In 2008 she received the Mother Seton Award from SOAR.

In 2011, The New Jersey assembly passed a resolution honoring Kathy's work with mothers and infants throughout New Jersey and poor inner city children who are "at risk" and children who are afflicted with AIDS (in Newark, NJ). Kathy was honored by the United Nations Women's Guild in Sept. 2013 for her loyalty and dedication to the service of mother-child care programs.

Several Sources Shelters is a non profit 501 CS and is completely privately funded. The proceeds of this book will help to operate their shelters, one of which is currently closed due to lack of funds. Donations are always welcomed and a blessing to our work for God's children in need.

In 2014 Kathy received the Pope John Paul II "Gravitas Award" from the RE:IMAGE Film Festival to recognizes the virtue of Gravitas in her efforts to communicate God's love through the use of the film "Gimme Shelter".

The Award is name after Blessed John Paul II who was also an actor and playwright. The Pope called artists to a higher order of responsibility because their gift come from God.

What is Several Sources Shelters?

When I first took in a pregnant teenager over thirty years ago, it was to help save the life of a pre born baby. Today we have grown to the point that we can reach out with God's love to so many more. We operate five shelters in New Jersey providing needed services for babies and their mothers, as well as for homeless women. We operate a national hotline (1-800-662-2687) which helps save preborn babies and brings hope-filled alternatives to frightened and desperate young mothers. We teach Holy Chastity, conduct Bible Study classes, and support our mothers and babies even after they leave our shelters through our Special Families "Care Packages" Program.

We assist others in their desire to open similar shelters by offering our free "How to Open a Shelter Kit" on our website. We offer compassion, hope, and love, so mothers and their babies in need of care are supported through God's mercy and understanding. Our benefactors have established an Educational Scholarship Program for our young mothers to go beyond high school. The presence and outreach of Several Sources Shelters is centered on the five shelters that we operate. They are beacons of light and hope for God's preborn and His children in need. Each of these homes is a safe haven for the lost and hurting mothers and their babies and the homeless women of the inner city of Newark.

Our Daytime Shelter in Newark, NJ helps the homeless women of Newark find permanent housing, dignity, food, clothing, and relief from the harsh and unsafe streets of the inner city as they rebuild their lives. They have a mailing address, a phone, computers, and spiritual and emotional support. Mothers also come with the children for a place to play away from the gangs. We exist to give them what they need to take the first step toward restoration: hope.

We provide free sonograms at "Our Gift of Hope" Sonogram Center. We overnight free pregnancy tests to young women to help them through an unplanned pregnancy anywhere in the U.S.A. and guide them to where they can also obtain free sonograms throughout the US. We also have Crisis Pregnancy Centers in the Ukraine and Uganda.

Become a Member of Our Several Sources Family and Help Keep Our Shelter Doors Open

Several Sources Shelters exists solely on the support and kindness of people who seek to reach out in compassion to God's children in need. If you would like to become a member of our Several Sources family, simply provide your mailing address and email and we will send you a copy of our most recent "Living Christmas Card" that tells the story of three of our young mothers and their babies. It also shows us celebrating Christmas with all of our mothers and their babies at our shelters. This ten minute DVD is a treasure for anyone who wishes to celebrate the gift of life. It can be used at youth groups and church activities to share the special joy of Christmas throughout the year. We will also include our Annual Christmas Ornament featuring the babies at our Shelters. No donation is necessary, but if you feel led, know it would be an answer to many mothers' prayers.

Write us at Several Sources Shelters, P.O. Box 157, Ramsey, New Jersey 07446 or email us at thebookinfo@severalsources.net. God bless you and thank you. Pray for us and know that we are always praying for you and your dear family. Kathy DiFiore, Founder of the Several Sources Shelters.

About the Film

Gimme Shelter releases on January 24, 2014.
Limited theater release.

Notes on Production from Kathy

When Ronald Krauss approached me in the winter of 2010 about the possibility of doing a documentary, I was taken aback and said "Absolutely no!" Being a filmmaker whose body of work focused on creating awareness for the needy, he had heard about Several Sources Shelters and the work I was doing. Ronald would not take no for an answer and was compelled to visit our shelter even if it was just to get a glimpse for his own eyes.

He didn't visit just once; he showed up repeatedly and began to document what he was seeing. Soon he became a regular and was well respected by the mothers. As he learned more and more, he saw the potential for a full-length feature film.

Ronald's interviews with the Several Sources mothers revealed things in their backgrounds that even I had not known. This was a sign of how much these girls trusted him and it made me reconsider the possibility that maybe there was a story Ronald could tell about the mothers and their struggles that could help many more who learned from their stories.

Soon Ronald's work of writing the script began. He moved into a small private area in one of our shelters and wrote based on his many interviews with me, my staff, and the mothers about life at the shelter over the course of a year. He followed the progress of young, abused and scared women who entered the shelter, seeing them transformed into beautiful, confident mothers with more clarity for their lives. This was to be the basis of his film.

When it came time to cast his lead role of Agnes "Apple" Bailey, Ronald made a very unusual decision in choosing to have the mothers at the shelter screen the actress auditions. He felt no one would know who was better to play is role than they would. He sent eight possibilities, and the girls were unanimous in their choice. This was also Ronald's first choice—Vanessa Hudgens. He now had his confirmation.

For Vanessa, landing the role was just the beginning of a long and challenging journey for her. Through Ronald's vision for the character, she gained fifteen pounds and chopped off all her hair. She wore a fake neck tattoo and several fake piercings. Her wardrobe consisted of baggy old clothes and worn-out shoes. In a bold effort to show her true determination and commitment, she moved into the shelter under our strict rules and guidelines for three weeks to learn more firsthand from the mothers and their lives. Living with the mothers and their babies took Vanessa to the deepest place of humility and prepared her with deeper understanding to tell their story prior to the filming of *Gimme Shelter.*

The rest of the cast was magnificent. Next we cast Brendan Fraser as Tom Fitzpatrick, Apple's biological father, whom she had never met due to his abandoning her pregnant mother. Brendan was so giving and caring. He could not do enough to help the mothers, the babies, and me every time we were in his company. He actually donated his entire salary for the film to the shelters on the final day of the shooting. This was truly an amazing surprise and showed what a blessing he was.

James Earl Jones who was cast as Father Frank McCarthy was so kind and interested in our work. He was beyond the perfect person to play the part! Actually, he was named after the priest who helped us to open our third shelter by letting us use his convent at Our Lady of Good Counsel Church for $1 rent a year!

Rosario Dawson took on the difficult part of Apple's mother. Again based on a true character, "June" is both a drug addict and prostitute with a violent past. She does such an amazing job in peeling back fragile layers of human emotion, giving us a realistic insight into the deep complexities of a troubled mother fighting for a second chance in life with her daughter.

Finally, we have Anne Dowd who plays Kathy. For me this was the most difficult part to cast. When was the last time someone was playing you in a film, putting your life and work on the screen? And for me it would be opening up old wounds from my past, dealing with things like abuse that I thought were far behind me. It turns out that it was a very healing experience, especially since this was my "crooked line" that God has used to help others. All of my friends and associates who have seen the film concur that Anne was the perfect choice in portraying me and capturing my style. Ronald had us working very closely together on the set and Anne was a sheer joy.

Four of the actual Several Sources mothers were in film. Twenty-four of our "saved" babies also appeared in the film. All of the scenes in the shelter were filmed on location at our Several Sources Shelters. The shooting included long and difficult hours beyond what I ever expected. I had no idea how grueling it could be, but it was worth every second because, as one of our mothers just emailed, "This movie is very special for us, not just because some of our babies are in it, but because it shares our story with the world. Just imagine, sharing with the whole world the sacred part of your life about what you went through just so you have your precious little angel by your side now."

People often ask me whatever happened to "Apple"—to the character. Where is she today? What is she doing? Apple's character was, in fact, based on two of the young mothers who were living at our shelters when Ronald Krauss, the director and producer, wrote the screenplay for *Gimme Shelter*. One young pregnant teen met Ronald at the shelter exactly on the day she had walked almost thirty miles in the middle of January to find us. Her name is Darlisha, and you will see her story in this book as well as her photos. She gave birth to her son, Julian, and went on to complete her diploma as a Certified Nurses Assistant, pass her driver's license test, and has made the decision to join our Several Sources Shelters staff as a full-time housemother. She will share her knowledge and serve as a role model for the other young mothers who enter our doors. She has become a permanent member of our Several Sources Family.

The other young mother who the Apple character is based on is the daughter of a Wall Street executive who, in the film, said to his daughter, "It's time to turn the page." This pregnant teen also came to live at our Several Sources Shelters. Dealing with an unplanned pregnancy was difficult for her and her family. Coming to our peaceful and nurturing Several Sources environment gave her and her loved ones the time necessary to heal their broken relationship. Soon after the baby was born, mother and little one both moved back to the grandparents' home. Anguish and strife became joy and celebration at the birth of a beautiful and precious granddaughter.

Ronald often told me that Apple was also based in part on many of the girls he had interviewed during his stay. There was a part of each and every one of them that touched him so deeply as they opened their courageous hearts to him in an effort to share their struggles and the abuse they all have endured, knowing it would help others. He often said to me, “These were the real heroes in life" as he would come out of each interview with tears in his eyes. Perhaps it takes one to know one. After all, he didn't have to live in a shelter, he volunteered, and now many lives will change because of it. God surely had a plan for us all.

That is what makes *Gimme Shelter* special. It shows how we can provide care to those most in need, and, with God’s help, how a mother and her love for her precious baby can endure all through the power of Hope, Faith, and Compassion.

> *Dear Lord, we pray that You, Lord, are pleased with Gimme Shelter. Please bless its message as it travels around the globe and please bless all of the mothers and their babies that need your help as they move forward to build lives*

together filled with Your Divine peace, joy, and love. AMEN.